# THE REJECTION CURE

# THE REJECTION CURE

## SOPHIE JONES

TONIC
LONDON • OXFORD • NEW YORK • NEW DELHI • SYDNEY

BLOOMSBURY TONIC
Bloomsbury Publishing Plc
50 Bedford Square, London, WC1B 3DP, UK
Bloomsbury Publishing Ireland Limited,
29 Earlsfort Terrace, Dublin 2, D02 AY28, Ireland

BLOOMSBURY, BLOOMSBURY TONIC and the Tonic logo
are trademarks of Bloomsbury Publishing Plc

First published in Great Britain 2026



A catalogue record for this book is available from the British Library

ISBN: HB: 978-1-0372-0205-6; eBook: 978-1-0372-0208-7;
audio: 978-1-0372-0207-0

2 4 6 8 10 9 7 5 3 1

Typeset by Six Red Marbles India
Printed and bound in Great Britain by Clays Ltd, Elcograf S.p.A

MIX
Paper | Supporting
responsible forestry
FSC® C018072
FSC
www.fsc.org

To find out more about our authors and books, visit www.bloomsbury.com
and sign up for our newsletters
For product-safety-related questions, contact
productsafety@bloomsbury.com

# CONTENTS

# INTRODUCTION

Towards the end of secondary school, I experienced a slow, subtle kind of bullying – not loud or obvious, but extremely isolating. I felt pushed out by the group, like I didn't belong, and that experience planted a very specific fear in me: the fear of group rejection. Not just one person saying no, but an entire circle turning against me. It made me question who I was and, worse, it made me start reshaping myself to fit in. I learned to read the room before I spoke, to shrink parts of my personality, to become whatever version of me seemed safest.

A few years later, I fell in love for the first time. We were together for two years, and I honestly thought I'd marry him. It felt like true love, and I threw myself into it – all heart, no safety net. When it ended, I was devastated. But more than that, I felt confirmed in all the fears I'd already been carrying – I wasn't good enough, people would leave, maybe if I were more likeable, more agreeable, more… something, they'd stay. Looking back, I can see how I chose to settle in this love because I had a core belief of not feeling good enough; I felt the need to chase this love, give too much, and overlook important aspects of the relationship that weren't working. But because I feared it was me that wasn't good enough, it felt easier to settle than leave the relationship. So I kept playing small, and no longer just in relationships but at work, too, as well as in how I expressed myself and the ways I moved through the world. I avoided anything that could lead to rejection, which meant I was holding back from experiencing the true essence and opportunities of life. And the funny thing is, I didn't even realise I had this fear until I landed my first ever corporate 'big-girl' job.

In May 2023 I was hired to be part of a gym's marketing team, as a social-media manager. I had no prior experience, but I knew I was good in front of the camera and had a lot of creative ideas. There was a constant turnover of new things to sell: the latest gym offers, personal trainer deals and shiny new gym kits. This meant we had a lot of marketing campaigns to produce.

My manager had an email chain where the whole marketing team could fire away any ideas they had for the latest campaigns. Her favourite phrase was 'no idea is a bad idea,' so it was a safe environment to throw in your suggestions. Everyone would fire up their ideas – except for me. Even though I knew I had some great ones on how they could market the new gym class, I just couldn't bring myself to share them. My worst fear was that they would be perceived as terrible and everyone would hate them. And if I ever did share my ideas, I felt like I was already compensating for an idea being disliked by adding, 'This may be a bad idea but…' Without realising it, I was discrediting myself and setting myself up to fail. I couldn't bring myself to share my thoughts with confidence. Then, one day, it clicked. I was sitting there, hesitating once again to speak up, to share an idea that I knew had value, and I asked myself … why? Why did something as simple as sharing a thought feel so heavy? So intimidating? That's when it hit me: I wasn't afraid of my ideas being bad, I was afraid of being rejected. Somewhere along the way, I started to believe that rejection wasn't just about my ideas being rebuffed; it reflected me as a person. Not getting validation felt like a direct dismissal of my worth, a shattering of my confidence, and an attack against my character. It wasn't just a no, it was 'you're not enough' and, though that realisation stung, it changed everything. Once I saw it clearly, I knew it was something I could challenge.

After becoming conscious of this fear, I started to notice the other areas where I was holding myself back out of fear of rejection. At the time, I found these to be profound revelations. For instance, I'd noticed that I wouldn't bother asking my friend if they wanted something as simple as chewing gum if I didn't think they did. Rather than asking (like any normal person would), I'd simply assume they didn't want any because I was afraid to ask. Another example: during the weekend I would bake delicious cupcakes that I spent hours on, preparing, perfecting, coming up with new flavours, but if I didn't think the people around me wanted any, I wouldn't bother to ask. Being faced with a 'no thank you' felt so crushing to me that I'd simply avoid broaching the subject!

This fear eventually snowballed into how I'd approach my friendships. I used to have a best friend growing up, all the way through primary school, and when both of us later attended the same secondary school, we were still incredibly close. But college was a fork in the road for us and we chose opposite paths. Our friendship started to change, we began to see each other less, and though I would think about her often, wondering if she would ever want to meet up, I avoided sending her a message. What if she ignored me? In the end, our friendship was never rekindled. I often wonder whether things could be different, but I've accepted, many years later, that we've gone our separate ways and there's nothing wrong with me cheering her on from a distance instead. Still, at the time, when I looked back on that moment, I began to realise that my fear of rejection was concerning. If it was stopping me from asking the simplest of questions, if it was stopping me from reaching out to friends, what other life-changing opportunities could I be missing out on?

One thing I knew for certain was that I had no idea how to cure my fear; it felt like something that was now part of me, an extra limb I'd have to live with. Besides, a fear of rejection wasn't a thing I'd heard anyone talk about overcoming; it was merely an unspoken anxiety that, it appeared, most humans struggled with, yet no one seemed to know how to manage it. But it got me thinking, and eventually, I did something about it.

# 1

# What is Rejection Therapy?

We've all been there. Rejected from a job we desperately wanted, turned down after the first date, being told 'no' when we ask for a pay rise, going in for a handshake and the other person not noticing, resulting in awkwardly trying to style it out. Having your optimism end in rejection can feel so deflating and embarrassing that it can even make us feel worthless, not quite 'good enough'; even when our loved ones tell us not to take it personally, we can't help but do that.

It's safe to say the feeling of rejection is unpleasant, and as a result we try to avoid it at all costs. But have you ever wondered how many opportunities, moments or connections you might have missed out on? Think about the friendships, career advancements, fun stories, or even whirlwind, epic-love journeys you could have experienced but haven't because fear held you back. We all have something we skipped out on because we didn't want to be knocked back – whether it's the job you never applied for, the question you never asked, the friendship that never blossomed, the trip you never took, or even the idea you never shared. All this boils down to one thing: the fear of rejection.

A fear of rejection isn't unusual; it affects most of the population, whether they're aware of it or not. This fear limits us from experiencing life to the fullest. It's that little voice in our head that says, 'Don't do that – what if I look stupid?' or, 'What if they don't want to meet up with me?' What if? What if? This subconscious fear becomes an obstacle in our lives more than we realise, but what if there was a way to overcome it? What if hearing the word 'no' was no longer so debilitating and instead became something you could shrug off with confidence? Well, this is where rejection therapy comes in. Think of this as the magic cure to be able to build resilience against rejection. By doing so, you can learn how to feel limitless. You'll realise that there's an abundance of opportunities that the world has to offer – all you have to do is ask.

One day, the penny dropped for me while I was scrolling through TikTok, watching a girl dance in the woods. I watched in awe; she seemed so cool, so confident. 'I'd like to do that,' I thought. But the only outdoor area near me – in the small town of Warrington – was my local park. After deliberating for a while, I thought to myself, 'No biggie, I'll go down there and have a go filming this TikTok dance outside.' Feeling optimistic (with little fear at this stage), I left for the park. It was completely full. Kids playing, people walking their dogs, families having picnics. The fear reared its ugly head and I wondered how in the world I'd be able to film my TikTok dance with all these people around. The thought of dancing in public and filming it sent me into an anxious frenzy. I wanted to do it so badly – just for a bit of fun – but almost instantly, I became stuck in my head again, struck with the fear of people watching me. The irony – that I was filming a video for TikTok which would potentially reach hundreds and thousands of people – wasn't lost on me. Yet there's something about being directly in front of strangers – a few kids and a few families and a few people walking their dogs – that felt much scarier. I'd be vulnerable, exposed to the people around me with nowhere to hide. A screen offered a safety blanket; I could retake and edit if needed and that gave me a level of control and security.

So I did what I believe most people would do and went to find a part of the park where I'd be less visible. A few minutes later, I was in a quiet location with no one around: no kids, no dogs, no families. I put my phone down and hit record. There was music playing from my phone; it was playing quietly so I could hear it for the moves I'd practised in my bedroom, but it wasn't playing loud enough for it to cause a scene. I started, but I was being small and shy with my movements. In my head I thought I would film my dance with energy and confidence but, in all honesty, I felt so self-conscious that I soon became bashful, small and timid. The fear shifted; now I was scared that someone would walk round the corner and catch me dancing on my own. That felt even more embarrassing. I kept trying to bring myself to have a boogie, but my body refused to respond. I left the park feeling deflated.

I recorded this whole anxious frenzy on my TikTok. I had the app open, already filming me the entire time, and when I realised I couldn't do it, I pressed 'record' again and started documenting how I was feeling instead. Watching this clip back now makes me anxious; I can still feel the fear radiating through the screen. I can't believe how nervous I was simply putting my phone down and recording myself, and, to be honest, the park wasn't even that busy! As you work your way through the book, you'll realise how much overcoming my fear of rejection has been transformed into confidence, but also how important it is to document this journey in your own way, so you can see your progress. Watching this video again, despite the initial feeling of anxiety, is always an amazing reminder of how far I've come.

As I'm documenting my freak-out on TikTok, at the end of the video I flippantly say, 'Maybe I should start an exposure therapy series.' At the time, I knew what exposure therapy was – a form of therapy where you purposely do something repeatedly that scares you, so your brain realises it's not actually scary, and you become desensitised to the fear it causes. It's a practice commonly used in cognitive behavioural therapy (CBT). I'd been interested in self-development at this point for around three years, using it as a tool to heal my own personal traumas. I found learning about how the mind works and how I can change it so incredibly fascinating that I was learning how to better myself near enough every day. I gained so much wisdom and knowledge that I decided to set up my TikTok account. My 'why' was to help at least one person, and when I came across rejection therapy, that, ultimately, seemed like the perfect next step of my development journey. Fast forward to the day in the park, and there I was, suggesting to my 4,000 TikTok followers that I should willingly do things outside my comfort zone to cure my social anxiety.

You may be thinking, 'But how does dancing in public correlate to the fear of rejection?' I thought the same thing, and that night I ruminated about why I cared so much about people watching me dance. After some time, I boiled it down to the fear of being judged. I didn't want to embarrass myself; I didn't want to feel public rejection.

That night, a girl popped up on my For You Page (FYP) on TikTok, asking a barista whether she could make her own coffee at a coffee shop. She referred to this action as 'rejection therapy'. I'd never heard of the concept before, but it made my skin crawl! 'I could never do that,' I said aloud from the safety of my living room. The coffee worker would think I was so entitled, that it was such a strange thing to ask. Still, I was curious, so I carried on watching. The girl in the video eventually explained that rejection therapy was a self-development challenge where you purposely seek rejection to embrace hearing the word 'no'. By intentionally seeking rejection and getting used to the awkward feelings that come along with it, you start to realise that the word isn't as bad as you think, and getting used to this can help you from holding yourself back. In a nutshell, the aim of rejection therapy is quite simple: ask questions that you know people are likely to say 'no' to.

Despite the initial skin-crawl, I was in awe of her confidence. Imagine being able to ask anything. And if the answer was 'no', it simply wouldn't bother you? Water off a duck's back! Imagine being able to shrug off the other person's possible judgements, and your own, and walk away not feeling embarrassed but, instead, empowered that you had had the courage to ask? That really appealed to me. That was a level of confidence I instantly dreamed of having. It got me thinking: if this rejection therapy scares me so much that it makes my skin crawl, clearly, I have a massive fear of rejection. Maybe it was something I should consider overcoming. I already knew my fear of rejection was impacting me; maybe this was what I needed to beat it.

## WHERE DID REJECTION THERAPY COME FROM?

Rejection therapy was founded by Canadian entrepreneur Jason Comely. An IT professional, Comely created rejection therapy as a social self-help card game to help people overcome their fear of rejection. The game was simple: intentionally seek rejection once a day for thirty days straight. Following on from this, it was the entrepreneur Jia Jiang who made this self-help game even more popular when he realised his fear of rejection was holding him back drastically in his career. He decided to take it up a notch and do one hundred days of rejection therapy. His results were so transformational that he did a TED Talk in 2016 to share how life-changing this 'game' can be. He went from being fearful to taking his career to the next level (all thanks to overcoming his fear of rejection). By embarking on a rejection therapy journey, he completely transformed his life and business for the better. He created a list of rejection therapy ideas for his one-hundred-day challenge, such as asking to borrow $100 from a stranger, asking to speak on the intercom at a shop, and even asking for a private jet (something I'm yet to do, but a girl can dream). It's wild how rejection therapy has gone from a niche challenge to a full-on trend. Watching so many people feel empowered to step outside their comfort zone and intentionally face rejection is genuinely life-changing. What started as an experiment by a male entrepreneur in his thirties has now grown into something bigger, and I'm proud to have taken it on as a young woman in my twenties. If it inspires just one more person to stop fearing the word 'no', then it's all worth it.

## WHAT'S THE SCIENCE BEHIND IT?

When I first started rejection therapy, I was worried that the amount of anxiety I felt wasn't normal, especially considering all I had to do was ask someone a question. So I went down a rabbit hole on the science of rejection therapy and why we all fear rejection. What I found was eye-opening.

Rejection therapy works because it's rooted in the science of exposure therapy, a proven psychological technique used to treat anxiety and phobias. By intentionally seeking out situations where rejection is likely, you repeatedly expose yourself to the very thing you fear, which gradually desensitises your brain's fear response, specifically located in the amygdala, two small, almond-shaped structures in the brain, primarily responsible for processing our emotions. Repeated exposure to rejection reduces the emotional sting of it over time, just like repeated weightlifting gradually allows you to go heavier and heavier. Psychologically, many of us struggle with high rejection sensitivity, which is often shaped by early experiences in childhood, and can lead to social anxiety, low self-esteem, and avoidance behaviours. And these behaviours can vary significantly, from not attending social occasions to not expressing your honest opinion, from declining invitations to no longer initiating plans with friends. Even things that don't have major stakes, such as not doing karaoke or entering talent shows when you were younger, to avoiding public speaking, and even avoiding eye contact! All these behaviours can be symptoms of fearing rejection. The rejection cure helps to break this cycle, training your brain to see 'no' not as a threat, but as feedback. Research also shows that people who face and push through rejection often build higher resilience and experience personal growth. Just like in exposure therapy, the key is starting small and building up – controlled, repeated exposure rewires your mindset and helps you respond to rejection with confidence instead of fear.

The fear of rejection is one of our most basic human fears; it evolved from the time when early humans depended on tribes for survival. Being part of a tribe meant access to food, comfort, community and resources. If you were rejected from the tribe for not acting like everyone else, or for having a different opinion, you would be kicked out, which meant no shelter, no food, no community, and simply an increased risk of death. So early on in our human development we learned to fit in for survival, and our brains learned to associate rejection with danger. We needed to blend in, and we needed to be liked if we wanted to survive.

Now this might have been helpful back in the days of tribal living, but as humans have developed and society has changed, we no longer need to indulge this same primal survival instinct. Admittedly, it's part of our evolution, so it's ingrained into our subconscious minds, which is why wanting to be liked is a default system within humans. Our brains don't enjoy being rejected. It's also why we don't like judgement. Subconsciously, when we're judged it makes our brain go into overdrive. We don't want to be disliked or misunderstood because it makes our brain think we're going to die. This is why office gossip, friendship drama, or even being huffed and puffed at by a stranger can send us into a big, overthinking panic. I used to feel so upset by road rage directed at me, for example. I could be waiting for the lights to change and not move quick enough, or accidentally take the wrong route and try to do a U-turn, and the feeling of anxiety I would get if I was beeped or snarled at could make me want to stop the car, get out and explain to them what had happened, or perhaps apologise, even when I didn't need to! The point is, it can be hard to shrug off injustice and the feeling of being judged while our brain is desperately trying to make us fit in. But simply being aware of this can make your brain fear rejection less and encourage you to dance to the rhythm of your own drum. The next time you find yourself holding back because of the fear of rejection, pause and ask yourself, 'Am I really at risk of being thrown out of a tribe?' Or, more bluntly, 'Will I die if I ask this question?' The answer is almost always 'no' and, sometimes, that simple truth is enough to put things into perspective and give you the courage to speak up.

# 2

# How to Do It

The fundamental rule of rejection therapy is to purposely seek rejection, but it's equally important to understand how to seek it, in order to do it properly. You want results that don't overwhelm your nervous system, or send your brain into panic mode, and don't make you give up after the first uncomfortable experience.

Our brain's primary job is to keep us safe, and as much as rejection can't physically hurt us, the moment we do a challenge that feels like too much of a leap, our brain interprets it as danger. That's why our palms sweat, our voice shakes, and we feel that growing pit in our stomach. It's our fight-or-flight response kicking in. If we skip ahead too fast – say, going from never asking for anything to asking your boss for a 50 per cent pay rise – we risk teaching our brain the wrong lesson: 'Rejection = danger.' And that's the opposite of what we want. Our goal is to re-educate the brain: 'Rejection = safe. I can survive it. And I can grow even stronger because of it.'

This is why the rejection cure needs to be gradual; think of it as strength training for your confidence. You don't start at the gym lifting a hundred kilos. You start small, build strength, and work your way up. Everyone's tolerance for rejection is different. What feels terrifying to me might feel like no big deal to you, and vice versa. So, when I say 'start small', I mean start small for you.

Small challenges can be as simple as asking your friends or family if they could give you a lift into town, if you could borrow an item of clothing, or even just asking to use a phone charger. The point is to progressively become more challenged and, eventually, ask bolder requests of strangers, such as going into a home store like IKEA and asking to have a nap on the beds, or going to a fire station and asking to slide down the pole, or requesting a shower in a bathroom showroom (cringey, I know!). The point is that you will be greeted with rejection.

When you start rejection therapy, it can quickly become clear that thinking of questions you're confident will get rejected isn't as easy as it seems. There are only so many times you can approach a family member asking if they would like some hand cream before you realise for this therapy to truly work, you need to get a little bold.

As someone who has personally embarked on this journey, let me give you a spoiler – **people don't like**

**to reject you.** Whether this varies by region, culture, or even gender, I can't say for sure. But from my experience as a girl living in the north of England, and having recently moved to the south, most people don't enjoy turning me down. Why? Because, at their core, people are generally kind. They know rejection stings, and often, they'd rather spare you that discomfort than outright say no. Yes, sometimes people will respond in a rude way – maybe they're confused by your request, caught off-guard, or simply don't know how to say no with kindness. And while that can feel intimidating, these moments are powerful milestones in your growth. Being rejected abruptly gives you the chance to prove to yourself that you can handle discomfort. Once your brain realises you've faced what you thought was 'the worst' – a bit of rudeness – and you're still standing, it begins to rewire your fear. You realise it wasn't as bad as you imagined and, with that, your resilience strengthens.

So this is where it gets fun (or anxiety-inducing). You need to think of questions that someone is pretty much forced into saying 'no' to. Some of my questions have been: asking for free petrol at a petrol station; asking for staff discount (in places where I do not work); and even asking if I can try on someone else's shoes in a supermarket. As you can imagine, the list is endless. The key point is, if you think the question will get you a 'no', go for it. Obviously, don't do anything illegal or inappropriate. This includes anything involving minors, stealing, or being straight-up rude (like gatecrashing someone's wedding). It's important that whatever you do is respectful and harmless to the other person involved.

It's also important to note that you will have to slowly build your resilience up by gradually making the challenges harder each time. I wouldn't recommend throwing yourself into the deep end with a bold challenge first, as you may be left feeling much more anxious than necessary. This challenge is designed so you can take slow, baby steps towards feeling invincible, all at your own pace. You'll learn more about this in the next chapter, which is all about getting started.

At this point you may be thinking: 'Why on earth would I put myself through that?' Maybe you're thinking that this whole thing is stupid, and you'll end up looking like an idiot. Well, yes, that is the whole point of doing rejection therapy – you're meant to feel silly and embarrassed. Rejection therapy teaches us about embracing those feelings rather than running away from them. By doing this, you'll learn to change your relationship with rejection and embarrassment, taking control and no longer letting fear rule. The more questions you ask, the more your brain starts to realise that getting rejected and receiving judgement can't hurt you unless you let it. It puts the power back in your hands and makes you realise that it's not the end of the world if someone gives you a funny look and says no.

Rejection therapy isn't just for someone wanting to transform their entire life, to become the next CEO or quit their job and travel the world (though it can help with this); rejection therapy can also improve your daily life. You'll no longer be apologetic about putting your ideas forward at work, or afraid to tell the barista your coffee order is wrong. You'll learn to go to the new gym class and stand at the front! You won't cringe about telling a potential romantic interest that you like them. You'll feel an entirely new-found confidence going about your daily business. Your work life will improve; you'll feel more secure in your relationships; you'll feel acceptance for who you are as a person, and no longer live your life in fear of everyone else's judgements and opinions because, fundamentally, you'll dance to the rhythm of your own drum and know that the only opinion of you that truly matters is yours.

**The rejection cure allows you to silence that inner critic in your mind.** The voice that says you can't do something; the voice that holds you back and tells you you're not good enough. We are much braver than we think, and doing rejection therapy will prove this to you. And it's not only me who thinks this; I've had hundreds of comments on my TikTok videos from the people who have embarked on their own rejection therapy journey, and it has changed their lives for the better too.

People have said to me:

- 'Wow, Sophie you really are changing my outlook on life.'
- 'Me and my boyfriend started doing rejection therapy this week and we can't believe how much it has grown our confidence already.'
- 'Whenever I feel nervous, I just ask myself: "What would Sophie do?" and it makes me feel a lot better.'
- 'I'm thirty years old and have never driven before but thanks to you, I'm starting driving lessons next week!'

Hearing comments like this makes my heart full. I started this challenge for my own growth but, through documenting my journey, I'm now able to help thousands of other people too.

Let's get started.

# 3

## Getting Started

So far, I've explored the concept of rejection therapy – how it can help you, what it teaches us, and how it can transform our relationship with fear. But ideas, no matter how inspiring, remain lifeless without action! This chapter is about bridging that gap: moving from theory to practice, from understanding to doing.

Think of this as the first real step into your rejection therapy journey. Up until now, you've been standing on the edge of the pool, dipping your toes in the water. Now it's time to wade in. But don't worry! You're not diving straight into the deep end. We'll begin small, with manageable actions and familiar faces, and build towards bigger challenges as your confidence grows. By the end of this chapter, you'll not only have a clear idea of how to start but also a road map for creating your own personal rejection therapy practice.

## STEP 1: PREPARING YOUR TOOLKIT

The first thing you'll need isn't bravery or even creativity; it's a notebook and a pen. This notebook will become your rejection therapy journal. It doesn't need to be fancy. What matters is that you use it as a companion on this journey.

Here's how to set it up.

### *1. First Page – Your Intentions*

Write down why you're doing rejection therapy. What do you hope to gain? More confidence? Less fear of what others think? The ability to handle discomfort without shutting down, feeling incredibly awkward lying in bed at night thinking about something you said?

For example:

- By the end of this journey, I want to feel comfortable asking for help when I need it.
- I want to stop letting the fear of embarrassment prevent me from trying new things.
- I want to build resilience so I can take bigger risks in my career.
- This isn't about getting it perfect; it's about setting a starting point.

*2. Second Page – How You Want to Feel*

Goals are often framed in outcomes (what we want to achieve), but rejection therapy is also about feelings. Write down how you'd like to feel when you've completed your first thirty days. Words like lighter, invincible, freer, stronger, bolder or more playful can be guiding stars when things feel tough.

*3. Ongoing Pages – Tracking Challenges*

After each rejection attempt, jot down what happened, how you felt before and after, and what you learned. This reflection will become a powerful reminder of your growth and show just how brave you are!

## STEP 2: STARTING SMALL – THE LOW-RISK ZONE

A great way to start is with people you already know – friends, family, colleagues. These are your 'safe spaces'. Yes, they'll probably say no. But their no won't sting quite as deeply because you already know that they care about you. When I first started practising rejection therapy, I asked my sister if she wanted to borrow my hairbrush. I asked my friend if they wanted chewing gum when I knew they didn't chew gum. I asked my mum if she'd like a lift to work even though she had her own car. These were tiny asks, but they gave me practice. I got to experience that little 'ouch' of rejection while still being grounded in the safety net of people who love me. Think of these people as your training wheels. They get you comfortable with the act of asking and with the mild discomfort of hearing 'no'. Once you have a few of these under your belt, you'll feel ready to step out into the wider world.

The temptation is to go big right away. Ask for a discount at a coffee shop, pitch an idea to your boss, or request something outrageous from a stranger. And while those are powerful exercises, they're not the best place to begin. Starting small matters. Like training a muscle, you build strength gradually. If you lift too much weight too soon, you risk injury. In rejection therapy, starting too big too fast can lead to discouragement.

Here are two simple, low-risk ways to begin:

- Ask a friend to lend you something trivial (like a pen or a phone charger). Even if they say no, the stakes are minimal.
- Make a playful request to a stranger, like 'Could you give me a high five?' or 'Could I take a selfie with your dog?'

The key is not whether they say yes or no – the power is in overcoming the fear and asking. Each small act trains your brain that you are much braver than you give yourself credit for, and you start to learn how to handle the discomfort of risk.

## STEP 3: EXPANDING THE CHALLENGE – A PROGRESSION LIST

As you grow more comfortable, it's time to expand, moving from safe people to mostly strangers. Don't worry, you don't have to launch into anything dramatic. Start with low-risk situations where the stakes are minimal and the interaction is fleeting. Below is a list of twenty suggested challenges, starting with low risk, moving through medium, and ending with high risk. Think of this as a buffet: you don't need to try everything, just pick one at a time.

*Low-Risk Challenges (Warm-Ups)*

1. Ask a stranger for the time (even if you have a watch or phone).
2. Hold eye contact with a shop worker and say, 'I hope you're having a great day.'
3. Ask for a free sample at a store that doesn't normally offer them.

4 Wear a brightly mismatched outfit in public.
5 Ask a friend if they'd like a lift to work.

*Medium-Risk Challenges (Stretch Zone)*

1 Ask a stranger to borrow their phone for a quick call.
2 Request a discount at a café or shop.
3 Sing or hum loudly while walking down the street.
4 Post something you normally wouldn't on your social media.
5 Give a compliment to a stranger – and then ask them for one back.

*High-Risk Challenges (Growth Zone)*

1 Ask a manager at a restaurant if you can help them serve tables for ten minutes.
2 Request an upgrade (at a hotel or on a flight).
3 Ask a street performer if you can join them for a minute.
4 Approach a group of strangers and ask to sit with them.
5 Share a personal story in front of an audience (open mic, class, meeting).

6 Ask your boss for a new responsibility at work.
7 Invite someone to lunch.
8 Walk into a high-end shop and try on something expensive.
9 Ask for directions to somewhere obvious (like the building you're standing in).
10 Email someone you admire, asking for advice or a short chat.

*Setting Boundaries*

One important note: rejection therapy should never be about being reckless, disrespectful, or intentionally making others uncomfortable. Notice that these questions still fall into the category of 'safe but unlikely'. You're not asking for anything harmful, rude, or truly disruptive. The key is keeping the rejection playful while allowing yourself to feel the discomfort. The point isn't to annoy people; it's to challenge yourself. Always use common sense, respect people's boundaries, and keep your challenges light-hearted. If you're ever unsure, ask yourself: Would I feel OK if someone made this request of me? If the answer is 'no', choose a different challenge. The questions aren't about tricking people or making them feel uncomfortable; they're about stretching your comfort zone. The likely outcome is a polite 'no', and that's the gold we're after. Here's the magic: you'll start to realise that 'no' isn't that bad. Most people are surprisingly kind when they say it. Often, they'll even smile, sometimes even apologise! And every time you survive a no, your brain updates its programming: 'I didn't die. Maybe rejection isn't so scary after all.' But always remember, the therapy is for you, but not at the expense of others.

### *Managing the Emotional Rollercoaster*

At this point, you'll start noticing the patterns in your body and mind. Maybe your heart races before you ask. Maybe you rehearse the words ten times in your head. Maybe you get shaky hands. That's normal. It's the body's way of saying, 'This feels risky.' The trick is not to fight those feelings but to accept them, embrace them, welcome them! You can do this by reframing them. Instead of telling yourself, 'I'm anxious', try 'I'm excited.' Physiologically, anxiety and excitement are very similar; both come with adrenaline, a fast heartbeat and increased energy. **Reframing can help you lean into the experience instead of shrinking away from it.** Breathing techniques are also incredibly helpful, and this will be your first most powerful tool. Before you make an ask, take one slow, deep breath, in and out. This calms your nervous system just enough to let you act despite the discomfort.

### *Rejection Logs: Tracking Challenges*

The second most powerful tool is to keep a 'rejection log' to track your progress. After each attempt, jot down:

1. What you asked for.
2. The person's response.
3. How you felt before, during, and after.
4. What you learned.

Over time, you'll see your progress in black and white. What felt impossible in week one will feel like no big deal by week four. If you want to skyrocket your confidence and get the most out of doing the rejection cure, I'd recommend starting with the thirty-day rejection therapy challenge: set out to get rejected daily, starting small and building it up. Soon enough, you'll notice something fascinating – the more you ask, the less attached you become to the answer. You start to realise that **rejection is just information, not a reflection of your worth.**

## STEP 4: CREATING YOUR OWN LIST

The above challenges are a starting point. Eventually, the real work comes from designing your own exercises. This way, they're tailored to your fears, your comfort zones and your growth edges.

Here's a framework to build your personal list:

- Five things you'd like to do in public (dance in a park, read aloud on the bus).
- Five silly things you'd like to try (wear sunglasses indoors, ask someone to sign your 'autograph book').
- Five things you'd never, ever do unless you were really brave (asking to drive a police car, pitching your wildest idea at work).
- Start with the first five. Work your way up. By creating your own ladder of challenges, you give yourself ownership of the process.

### *The Surprising Yes*

Here's another bonus: sometimes you'll get a 'yes', and those yeses can be life-changing. The more you ask, the more opportunities you stumble upon that you never would have had otherwise. The more some of your questions become tailored to things you genuinely want to do for the fun of it, or the challenge, or the experience, outside of just mastering the acceptance of the word 'no'. I've had people say 'yes' to me walking their dog, having coffee together, making my own ice cream in an ice-cream van, making my own pizza at a pizza takeaway, and the biggest one was asking to go on a national radio station – all of them said 'yes'! Getting a yes never fails to blow my mind; not only is it extremely liberating and fun, but it also opens your mind up to the number of opportunities that are out there in life. And as much as these seem like harmless 'yes'es – as in they're fun but not going to change your life, the actual whole magic is, if you know you can get a 'yes' for trivial things, how many things can you get a 'yes' for that you actually care about once you have the courage to ask? It shows you that people are very willing to say 'yes' to you if you come across with good intentions and positive vibes.

Now imagine this could happen to you! Asking for a tour of a kitchen and being shown around by the chef. Or asking for a discount and getting one. Or asking a stranger for advice and receiving wisdom that sticks with you for ever. These surprises are the icing on the cake of rejection therapy. You weren't asking for the 'yes', but sometimes it shows up anyway.

## STEP 5: THE POWER OF GOAL-SETTING

Without clear goals, rejection therapy can feel random. You might complete challenges but, without direction, you risk missing the deeper transformation. Goals act like a compass, keeping you on track.

Remember to go back from time to time to the first page of your notebook, and remind yourself why you're doing this. You can also do regular check-ins with yourself, asking:

- What do I want to achieve by the end of this journey? (Confidence, resilience, playfulness?)
- What is one concrete outcome I'd like to see? (Speaking up in meetings, asking for a raise, joining a community group?)

For example, when I first began, my goal was simple: I wanted to see what could happen to my confidence if I repeatedly pushed myself out of my comfort zone. I wanted to see what might happen with my job, how my friendships might expand, whether I'd one day have the courage to move away (spoiler – I did!). Without that goal, I would have given up when I felt uncomfortable. With it, I kept plodding forward, even when things became hard and the sense of discomfort began to mount.

### *Handling Discomfort*

Rejection therapy isn't about avoiding discomfort; it's about leaning into it. The discomfort you feel before or during a challenge is the signal you're in the right place.

Remember the powerful tools to handle that discomfort:

- Breathe through the nerves – Pause, take three deep breaths, and notice how your body relaxes.
- Reframe the 'no' – Instead of 'I failed', think 'I practised courage.' Instead of 'I'm scared', think 'I'm excited.'
- Celebrate attempts, not outcomes – Success is measured by asking, not by the answer you receive.

Discomfort is temporary, but the growth you build by facing it lasts. The reflection part of this journey is the secret ingredient; always remember to fill in your rejection log. Many people skip this step. They try challenges, get rejected, and then move on without processing the experience. **Reflection is where the gold is found.** Over time, you'll notice patterns: maybe rejection isn't as painful as you thought, or maybe people are kinder than you imagined. This awareness reinforces your courage.

*Start Today!*

This chapter is your invitation to begin – not someday far in the distance, but today. Get a notebook, write down your intentions, choose a challenge, and take the first step. The rejection cure isn't about collecting 'no's for their own sake. It's about training yourself to live boldly, free from the invisible fences of fear. Each small rejection makes the next one easier, and each act of courage builds momentum for the next. Remember: you're not aiming for perfection. You're aiming for progress. And every 'no' you receive is proof that you're showing up for yourself in a way that most people never will.

You've got this... deep breath.

# 4

## Reframing Fear

When I first started practising rejection therapy, the fear of a challenge would eat me up all day. I would procrastinate – putting it off because it scared me so much. For the first ever challenge that I filmed, I was at an amateur theatre production and had decided that at the end of the show, I was going to ask someone that worked there whether I could sing with the band. In hindsight, after every challenge I've done, this seems so easy, but at the time I was mortified. It meant that I didn't enjoy the show, since all I could think about the entire time was how I was going to ask if I could sing with the band at the end, who I would ask, when I would ask it – before or after introducing myself? – and what they were going to say. I was scared of being judged, of people thinking I was entitled; it was the performers' big day, not mine, yet here I was asking if I could steal the limelight and sing with the band. The fear boiled down to this: being perceived in a way that I wouldn't want people to perceive me, and that inability to control their perception was frightening.

The end of the show came and with it, the moment to ask. The tension had been building up, and I was riddled with nerves. My hands felt clammy and the applause seemed louder than it probably was, ringing in my ears. But I had set myself the challenge and I was determined to push myself out of my comfort zone and complete it. I approached a lady working at the show. 'Hi. Can I sing with the band?' I asked. Her reaction wasn't what I was expecting. She stuttered, looking around as if to ask her colleague what to do. She seemed (naturally) confused, but she was kind, she smiled and she didn't make me feel silly. It was like she didn't want to let me down. 'Maybe if you find the manager and ask them?' she said. Can you imagine! In the end I couldn't find the manager, plus the thought of having to ask someone again was awful. A win is a win, I thought. I still asked and the response was still a gentle type of 'no', so, technically, mission success. You might be thinking, was that even worth it? Getting all nervous, not enjoying the night and ultimately feeling silly? But this is the interesting part – I felt so liberated after I had asked. I felt so proud of myself for doing something I was nervous about. I left the theatre on a high.

That feeling of liberation is what rejection therapy is all about. It's not really about whether you get a direct 'yes' or a 'no', though that 'no' is an important word to get used to; it's about facing the fear that tells you not to do it in the first place. The fear before doing the challenge is often worse than the challenge itself. It's the anticipation, the endless 'what if's that run through your head, the stories your mind invents about how terrible it might be, that truly keep you from doing anything at all. But once you take that step, something magical happens: your brain realises that you didn't die. You didn't lose your dignity. You didn't implode from embarrassment. You survived and, more often than not, you even feel good afterwards.

Overcoming the fear before rejection therapy is the hardest part for most people. Getting to the point where you can face the fear, where you can stop overthinking, stop freezing, and actually do the thing is a key next step in the rejection cure. Here's how to work through it.

## 1. RECOGNISE THE VOICE OF FEAR

Before every rejection challenge, there's a voice that will try to talk you out of it. It's sneaky, convincing and sounds very logical. 'Maybe today's not a good day… You're too tired… This one doesn't count, you can skip it.' That's fear, believe it or not, trying to protect you. It's your brain doing what it's evolved to do, keeping you safe from potential threats. The only problem is, your brain doesn't know the difference between a lion chasing you and a barista possibly saying 'no' to your weird request for a free coffee refill.

When this fear shows up, don't fight it or try to suppress it. Instead, notice it. Say to yourself, 'Ah, there's that voice again.' Acknowledge it with compassion. You can even thank it: 'Thanks for trying to protect me, but I'm safe.' That small mental shift reminds you that fear isn't the truth; it's just an emotion. **It's how you choose to react to that emotion that makes a difference.**

### 2. THE 'ARE YOU GOING TO DIE?' TECHNIQUE

One of the simplest and most effective tools for overcoming fear before a challenge is to ask yourself the brutally honest question: Am I going to die?

It sounds dramatic but it instantly cuts through the noise. When you think about it, most fears we have around rejection therapy are social: fear of embarrassment, judgement, awkwardness, or being seen in a negative light. None of those things are fatal. The worst-case scenario usually ends with you feeling uncomfortable for about thirty seconds. That's it. Every time your brain catastrophises the outcome – 'They'll think I'm crazy!... People will laugh!... I'll make a fool of myself!' – respond with: 'Am I going to die?' The answer is always no. And that realisation can give you the courage to move forward, because if you're not going to die, you can handle whatever comes your way.

## 3. REFRAMING THE FEAR: IT'S NOT ABOUT THE RESULT

Most of the fear before doing a rejection challenge comes from focusing on the result: 'What if they say no? What if they laugh at me?' But the rejection cure isn't about the result. It's about the process, about intentionally facing the discomfort to reach a new state of confidence, of self-assuredness. Once you reframe success as asking, not receiving, fear loses much of its power. The goal is simply to put yourself out there. Whether you get a 'yes' or a 'no' doesn't matter, because both outcomes are valuable. A 'yes' feels great, but a 'no' is where growth happens.

**The most freeing thing you can tell yourself before a challenge is: my success depends on me asking, not on what happens after.** Soon, this will start to apply to life in general. My success depends on me trying, not on the outcome... My success depends on me giving it a go, not whether I win or not... My success depends on me, not the opinions of others.

## 4. THE FREEZE RESPONSE AND HOW TO BREAK IT

Let's talk about the 'freeze'. You know the feeling: your body tightens, your heart races, and your mind blanks. You want to move, but it feels impossible. You're a deer caught in the headlights, fatally stopped in your tracks. This is a biological reaction. When your body perceives a threat, like potential social rejection, your nervous system enters fight, flight or freeze mode.

The good news is you can train your body to move through that freeze. The trick is to take small, deliberate, physical actions. Movement interrupts the freeze response, reminding you that you have other choices. Try these three simple steps:

1. **Take one deep breath.** Inhale for four seconds, hold for two, exhale for six. This signals safety to your body. The reason why deep breathing is such a valuable tool is because it reminds your body that you are safe. If you were in actual danger (which your body thinks you are), you wouldn't have time to stand there and take a deep breath, so deep breathing sends safety signals to your brain and calms the nervous system down.
2. **Smile.** It might feel forced, but it tells your brain that things are OK. The endorphins released

from smiling, whether it's from genuine feelings of happiness or not, are real. Endorphins are natural mood-boosting and pain-relieving chemicals that can flood your brain when you smile, creating a positive feedback loop, where the physical act of smiling can actually make you feel happier and more relaxed by stimulating the body's reward system.

3 **Take one small action.** If your challenge is to ask a stranger a question, don't think about the entire interaction. Just think, 'I'll take one step towards them… I'll count down from three…' Once you start moving, the rest follows naturally.

This is a technique that helps me a lot. Once, when I was sitting on my sofa at home, I had planned to paint my face bright green and walk to the shops as a way of practising rejection therapy. I was procrastinating because of my nerves, but I found that by taking one small action rather than staying glued to that sofa, festering in my own thoughts, helped get the ball rolling. I stood up, which meant I left the room; I walked upstairs, which led to me getting changed; then I packed my bags, and finally, I painted my face and left. This entire stream of small conscious doing took me out of a thinking spiral and into a chain of action.

Now, one of my favourite phrases is 'don't think, just do'; it's a call to push past the lingering hesitation, embrace the challenge ahead (big or small), and persist through perceived setbacks.

**Action kills anxiety, while fear thrives on hesitation.** The moment you start moving, even just one small step, the fear loses its grip.

## 5. MAKE A PRE-CHALLENGE RITUAL

Rituals have power. They signal to your brain that you're entering a safe, familiar pattern, even if the task ahead is uncomfortable. By reducing the activity in your amygdala, the part of the brain responsible for threat detection, your stress and anxiety alerts are lowered. Before doing a rejection challenge, create a short ritual that grounds you. The repetitive nature of the task, whether that's journalling, breathwork, repeating an affirmation, smiling or visualisation, creates an arena of predictability and emotional regulation, allowing you to stay calm as you dive into the task ahead.

When you repeat this ritual before each challenge, your brain begins to associate it with courage, resilience and reward. Over time, the fear decreases because the ritual itself becomes a comfort cue.

## 6. REWARD YOURSELF, ALWAYS

This is a huge one. Reward yourself after every rejection challenge, no matter how it goes. You deserve it, not for getting a 'yes', but for taking action despite the fear.

The reward doesn't have to be grand: it can be something small, like a sweet treat or your favourite coffee, or simply saying aloud: 'I'm proud of myself.' The key is to reinforce the behaviour through positive reinforcement, which is a key determiner in long-term behavioural changes. **Your brain learns through reward loops, and when you reward yourself after doing something scary, your brain starts to associate facing fear with positive feelings.**

When I first started my rejection journey, the nerves were high but, afterwards, I would always give myself a reward. Try this: make a list of twenty things that feel like a reward for you. It could be calling a friend for an hour just to chat, a solo cinema date, buying your favourite sweet treat, going on a bike ride, buying that new pair of shoes you saw last week, or running yourself a nice warm bath. On the bigger scale, maybe it's booking yourself a day trip somewhere, buying a theatre ticket to an upcoming show, or adding more books to your ever-growing TBR pile. Whenever you finish a task, come back to this list and select, at random or specifically, a reward for yourself. The rewards remind you how brave you can be, and that the challenge probably wasn't as bad as you thought.

Over time, rewards rewire your response. Instead of associating rejection with pain, your brain begins to associate it with pride, joy and empowerment. So don't skip the reward – it's one of the most powerful psychological tools you have.

## 7. SEPARATE THE STORY FROM THE REALITY

Fear thrives on stories. The 'film' that plays in your head of everything that could go wrong has a full cast, the best lighting, even a sequel. But most of the time, these stories never happen. Before your next challenge, take a minute to write down two things:

1. The story your brain is telling you. 'They'll think I'm weird, I'll embarrass myself, everyone will stare.'
2. What's actually happening. 'I'm asking a simple question that anyone could ask. If they say no, life goes on.'

When you compare those two summaries, the fear starts to lose its power and the story soon becomes boring. You realise how exaggerated it really is, how poor the acting, how melodramatic the dialogue. This simple exercise helps you return to reality, and reality is rarely as scary as your imagination.

## 8. THE POWER OF SELF-COMPASSION

We often think bravery means being fearless. But real bravery is feeling terrified, doing it anyway, and being kind to yourself throughout. There will be days when you freeze, when you bail on a challenge, when the fear wins. That's OK. Beating yourself up doesn't make you braver; it just makes you dread trying again. Self-compassion keeps you in the game. Treat yourself like you'd treat a close friend who's scared; you'd never call them weak or stupid for feeling anxious. You'd say, 'That was hard, but I'm proud of you for even thinking about doing it.' Talk to yourself the same way.

Once, when I was trying to do funny walks across the road when the lights went red and cars would stop, I physically couldn't do it. I beat myself up about it, but I shouldn't have because it wasn't a failure. It's never a failure. It's about having the courage to try, and maybe that challenge is a little bit too hard at the moment, but one day you'll feel brave enough to do it and you'll feel even prouder of how far you've come.

## 9. PRACTISE MICRO-COURAGE

You don't have to start with huge, terrifying challenges. Courage is a muscle, and like any muscle, it strengthens gradually. Start with micro acts of courage:

- Make brief eye contact with a stranger.
- Ask a cashier how their day is.
- Compliment someone in public.
- Ask for a small favour you'd normally avoid.

These tiny acts may seem insignificant, but they build momentum. Each small victory teaches your brain that discomfort is survivable. Eventually, you'll be able to take on bigger and bolder challenges without feeling paralysed by fear.

## 10. VISUALISE THE AFTER-FEELING

When you're standing on the edge of a challenge, fear makes you focus on the before: the anxiety, the racing heart, the dread. Instead, shift your focus to the after. Visualise how good you'll feel once it's over: the relief, the pride, the sense of accomplishment. That post-challenge high is powerful. It's the emotional reward that keeps people coming back to rejection therapy. The more vividly you can imagine that feeling, the easier it is to push through the initial fear.

## 11. CREATE A 'FEAR-TO-ACTION' RULE

To prevent overthinking, which is a natural loop our brains can get stuck in just before taking action (like I did when I was sitting on my sofa, wondering whether to go out with my face painted green or not), make a rule: when you feel fear about a challenge, you have ten seconds to start moving. Ten seconds to short-circuit your hesitation.

The longer you sit with fear, the louder it gets, but when you act within a short window, you catch your brain before it can talk you out of it. Sometimes, counting down from ten, or five, or three, is enough action in itself to shift your brain into action mode. As soon as you feel that surge of anxiety, begin to count down and move. The action doesn't have to be the full challenge. It could just be walking towards the person or opening your mouth to speak, but once you've started, your brain has no choice but to follow through.

## 12. COLLECT EVIDENCE THAT YOU CAN HANDLE IT

Every time you complete a rejection challenge, even if it goes terribly, write down what happened and what you learned – about yourself, about your body, about the recurring thoughts the voice in your head keeps repeating. Over time, you'll build a library of evidence proving that you can handle fear, and you'll be able to notice the patterns in your own anxiety. You'll notice that the fear before is always worse than the experience itself. Seeing that pattern written out helps retrain your mind. Next time you start to panic, remind yourself, 'I've done this before, and it wasn't as bad as I imagined.'

The beauty of overcoming fear in rejection therapy is that it doesn't just help you with rejection; it transforms your whole life. You start to realise how much fear is used to control your decisions, how much it's been holding you back in conversations, in relationships, in career opportunities. You begin to see fear for what it really is: a signal that you're about to expand your comfort zone. And the more often you face it, the more freedom you feel.

**Every time you face rejection, you chip away at the invisible wall that holds you back from living fully.** You'll realise that fear isn't an enemy to fight, but a compass pointing to growth. The more you walk towards it, the more confident, courageous and alive you'll feel.

So next time that familiar dread creeps in, remember:

- Fear is a sign you're doing something meaningful.
- You won't die!
- The after-feeling is always worth it.
- Reward yourself!

Every 'no' brings you one step closer to total freedom, the kind of freedom that only comes from realising that you can handle anything, if not most things, including rejection.

# 5

# Overcoming Fear of Judgement

For many, the real fear behind rejection is not the 'no' itself, it is the fear of being judged. The moment you imagine asking for something and being told no, your mind instantly fills with images of how others will see you. Will they think you're weird? Entitled? Too much? Not enough? This is the emotional core of rejection therapy, because every time you put yourself in a situation where you might be rejected, you're also putting yourself in a position to be judged.

The rejection cure is about learning to stand in that moment of discomfort, to face the possibility of judgement and realise that even when people form opinions about you, you are still safe, whole and worthy. The practice forces you to look your deepest social fears in the eye and see that they are not as powerful as you once believed. If someone says no to your request, you start wondering what they might have thought about you, whether they'll be talking about you later, negatively, to their friends. This fear keeps most people from even trying. It's why you might spend all day building up the courage to ask a simple question in a rejection challenge. You're not fighting the possibility of rejection; you're fighting the possibility of being perceived in a negative way. Rejection therapy works because it brings this fear into the light. Instead of hiding from judgement, you walk directly into it. Each challenge gives you a chance to feel the discomfort, to notice that nothing truly bad happens, and to realise that most people are kinder and more understanding than you expected.

## THE POWER OF EXPOSURE

Rejection therapy is exposure therapy for social fear. Every time you put yourself in a situation where someone could say 'no', you are retraining your brain. You are teaching your nervous system that being judged or rejected is not a threat to your safety. The first few times, it feels awful. You might overthink every detail, play the situation in your head a hundred times, or even try to talk yourself out of doing it. But each time you go through with it, something begins to shift. The intensity of the fear starts to fade. You learn to recover faster. You realise that most of the judgement you feared was in your own mind.

When you experience rejection and survive it, your brain begins to rewire itself. You start to understand that judgement and rejection do not define you. You define you. That is the hidden gift of rejection therapy: it builds a kind of unshakeable confidence that cannot be taught through theory, only through experience.

## CHILDHOOD CONDITIONING AND THE FEAR OF BEING SEEN

Many people trace their fear of judgement back to childhood. From a young age, we learn that approval equals love and acceptance. When we are praised, we feel safe and valued. When we are criticised, told off, laughed at or embarrassed, we feel exposed and alone. Over time, this trains the brain to associate being judged with pain.

You might remember moments where you raised your hand in class and gave the wrong answer and everyone laughed. Or times when you expressed yourself honestly and someone said you were too much, too sensitive. Those memories stick. They become silent rules you live by: stay small, stay agreeable, stay invisible.

Rejection therapy challenges those rules. It asks you to take up space again, to speak, to ask, to risk being seen. It invites you to meet the part of yourself that still feels like that little kid who just wants to fit in. Every time you do a rejection challenge, you are showing that inner child that it is safe to be visible now. You are the adult in control, and you can handle whatever comes your way.

## SOCIETY, COMPARISON, AND THE WEIGHT OF EXPECTATIONS

Modern society has amplified the fear of judgement through constant comparison. Social media has become a global stage where everyone appears confident, successful and flawless. We compare ourselves to these curated versions of others and fear that we will never measure up. This is why rejection therapy is such a powerful tool, particularly today. When you deliberately put yourself in situations where you might be rejected, you begin to see how unrealistic those expectations are. You realise that everyone is simply doing their best, and that the curated lives we see on social media, day in, day out, are simply that: tailored, managed, built on the fear of rejection and, therefore, fuelling unrealistic expectations about how to live.

The more rejection therapy you do, the more you start to care less about image and more about experience. What is it to live your life to the fullest? What is something that you'd love to do that feels silly, would seem crazy, would devastate you if it didn't work? Those are the experiences we should be chasing after, not how many likes or comments we can get.

Instead of trying to appear perfect, it's time to start valuing authenticity. It's time to stop living for approval and start living for growth.

## PROJECTION AND PERSPECTIVE

When someone judges you, it's often a projection of their own insecurities, fears and beliefs. If someone criticises you for being bold, it might be because they wish they could be as courageous. If they say you're strange, it might be because they're uncomfortable with their own uniqueness.

Rejection therapy gives you constant opportunities to witness this in action. When someone reacts negatively, you begin to realise that their response says more about their inner world than about your worth. You start to care less about pleasing everyone, and more about being authentic.

Over time, you build resilience by separating your identity from other people's opinions. You can respect their perspective without taking it personally, and this mental shift is where real freedom begins.

## THE TURNING POINT: WHEN JUDGEMENT LOSES POWER

The most transformative moment in rejection therapy often comes after a rejection that once would have crushed you. You ask for something outrageous, get a flat-out 'no', and instead of shrinking, you find yourself smiling. You feel free. Why? Because you finally see that you can survive it. Judgement no longer has the power to paralyse you. It might still sting for a second, but it no longer defines your choices. When you reach this point, life opens up. You stop waiting for permission. You take risks, speak up, and show your real personality. You no longer need to control how others see you because you are too busy living.

If external approval cannot be your foundation, what can? The answer is internal validation, learning to approve of yourself – measuring your worth based on your own values, not on other people's opinions. It means being proud of yourself for showing up, trying, and staying true to what matters to you, even if others do not understand.

To build it, try these practices:

1. **Define your own metrics for success.** Ask yourself what truly matters to you. What makes you feel proud, fulfilled, or aligned with your values? Separate this into three columns and list five things in each. When you know your values, other people's opinions lose their power.
2. **Practise self-acknowledgement.** Each day, note one thing you did that reflects courage, kindness or authenticity. It could be something as small as speaking up in a meeting or saying 'no' when you wanted to say 'yes'. If there's more than one thing, even better, but write it down.

3 **Create an internal cheerleader voice.** That inner critic will always find reasons to doubt you. Counter it with an internal voice that celebrates you, the voice that says, 'I am proud of myself for being me… I put myself out there… I am capable of whatever I set my mind to.' Internal validation doesn't mean you stop caring about others altogether. It means your peace no longer depends on their approval.

## REFRAMING JUDGEMENT AS NEUTRAL

Part of overcoming the fear of judgement is learning to see it as a neutral event. Judgement is not inherently good or bad; it simply exists. People have opinions the way they have favourite foods. Rejection therapy helps you practise this reframe in real time. When someone says 'no' or looks at you strangely, you can remind yourself that they're just processing. It doesn't mean you're wrong for asking; it doesn't even mean they've thought about or considered in depth the reaction they're having; it is simply that: a reaction.

Once you stop labelling judgement as a threat, it loses its emotional charge. You begin to experience rejection with curiosity instead of fear. You might even start to enjoy the process of seeing how different people react.

## THE FEAR OF BEING MISUNDERSTOOD

One of the hardest parts of judgement is being misunderstood. You know your intentions are good, but someone interprets them the wrong way. This can be especially challenging during rejection therapy, when your requests may seem unusual or unexpected and your worst nightmare would be to ruin someone's day, or make someone feel uncomfortable.

In these moments, it helps to remember that being misunderstood is not failure. It is part of being human. No one can fully understand another person's motives or experiences. By following through with the rejection cure, you learn to tolerate being misunderstood and hope that, in turn, you can free others from feeling misunderstood too. You realise that you don't need everyone to 'get' you. The people who are meant for you will appreciate your courage, honesty and authenticity.

Not all judgement is harmful, either. Constructive criticism can help you grow if you receive it without defensiveness. Rejection therapy trains you to listen to feedback with clarity and become better at distinguishing between constructive input and unhelpful projection. If someone says 'no' to your request and offers a reason, you can reflect on it without shame. Maybe it teaches you something valuable about communication, timing or empathy. This mindset transforms rejection into a teacher rather than an enemy. You begin to see every judgement, whether fair or not, as an opportunity to understand yourself and others more deeply.

## THE FREEDOM OF AUTHENTIC LIVING

As you continue with the rejection cure, you will naturally begin to live more authentically. You will no longer hide behind the fear of what others might think. You'll say yes to opportunities, share your ideas, and express your true personality. Authenticity attracts the right kind of people into your life – those who appreciate you for who you are rather than who you pretend to be. The more authentic you become, the less judgement affects you, because you are no longer performing. You are simply being. It is better to be rejected for who you really are than to be accepted for a version of yourself that feels false.

## STEPS TO HEAL FEAR OF JUDGEMENT: THE 'SO WHAT?' TECHNIQUE

Something I love to use to help my fear of judgement is the 'so what?' technique. When your mind spirals about what people might think, ask 'So what?'

- What if they think I'm weird? So what?
- What if they think I'm not qualified? So what?
- What if they think I'm too much? *So what?*

Asking yourself 'So what?' instantly cuts the drama and grounds you in perspective, taking the power away from possibly getting judged. The more you practise rejection therapy, the more it will help you overcome your fear of judgement, as you quickly realise that what people think of you can't hurt you – knowing that is liberating.

Imagine waking up and realising that judgement no longer controls your life. You speak freely; you take chances; you post online; you follow your curiosity without second-guessing yourself. You quit your job and start that degree you've been thinking about; you move countries to learn a new language; you ask that person you've been crushing on for weeks, maybe months (maybe years!), on a date; you put in a request to speak with your manager about a promotion you've been waiting too long for; you apply for a completely different role, in a completely different company, because you no longer care that there might be more qualified candidates than you. That is the freedom rejection therapy leads to. You still notice judgement, but it feels distant. It no longer dictates your choices. You might even smile at it, knowing it once ruled your world but no longer does.

Rejection therapy teaches you that the opinions of others are just noise compared to the clarity of your own voice. Judgement might be unavoidable, but it doesn't have to be a barrier, and the real question is whether you'll let it silence you or strengthen you. Through rejection therapy, you learn that every 'no', every judgement, and every uncomfortable moment is a doorway to liberation. Each time you face the fear and act anyway, you reclaim a piece of yourself that once hid away for safety.

When you stop giving your power to other people's opinions, life opens up in the most beautiful way. You laugh louder, try more, and live unapologetically as yourself.

So, the next time you fear being judged, remember that fear is only old survival tactics from a time when belonging meant life or death. Today, you belong to yourself. And that is the greatest freedom of all.

# 6

## How to Stop Wearing the Mask

We all have a version of ourselves that we present to the world. It's the subconsciously curated image we hope others will see – polished, likeable, confident and put-together. Some may call it an ego, but it's really protection. This version of ourselves we project externally isn't an honest depiction of the multifaceted individuals we truly are, but we hope that it's enough to get us by, day to day. It's a carefully constructed mask, woven from years of experience, a feedback loop in our minds, and silent decisions about who we're supposed to be.

The mask helps us feel safe, protecting us from judgement, embarrassment or the possibility of rejection. But it also keeps us confined, because whenever we act in a way that doesn't align with that carefully managed identity, when we say something spontaneous, take an unexpected risk, or do something 'out of character', our internal alarm bells go off. Suddenly, the nervous system lights up, our heart races, our chest tightens, and the mind scrambles to make sense of it.

We feel the urge to explain ourselves, to justify why we acted that way, to quickly repair the crack in our protective shield before anyone notices.

That discomfort isn't just emotional – it's biological. Our brains are wired to predict social outcomes, and when we step outside our usual pattern of behaviour, the brain loses its familiar script, and that unpredictability feels dangerous. It's the same primal instinct that once warned our ancestors to stay close to the tribe, because being cast out meant real physical risk. Today, rejection doesn't mean being left to face wild animals but, to our nervous system, it can feel just as threatening.

This constant need to maintain our image shows up subtly in daily life. We bite our tongue in conversations because we don't want to sound silly. We overthink text messages, wondering if we came across the wrong way. We agree to things we don't truly want, just to avoid seeming difficult. We post online versions of ourselves that look calm and confident, even when inside we're overwhelmed and burning out. Each of these small, seemingly harmless acts reinforces the same message: it's safer to be accepted than to be authentic.

The problem is, living this way, from the ego instead of the heart, slowly disconnects us from who we really are. The ego's job is to protect, not to express. It tries to manage how others see us, but in doing so, it dulls our sparkle and our true connection to feeling alive. When we're overly concerned with maintaining an image, we stop listening to our feelings and desires. Instead, we start to shape our decisions around what will look good, sound good, or be well received, rather than what feels true. Over time, this can lead to exhaustion, anxiety and even resentment towards those we love, or careers we care about – even ourselves, because, deep down, we know we're hiding.

On the surface, rejection therapy almost sounds counterintuitive. Why deliberately seek rejection and intentionally put yourself in situations where people might say no or misunderstand you? Because beneath the challenge lies a deeper lesson. Rejection therapy isn't just about the 'no'; it's about what happens inside you when you are seen in a way you didn't plan to be seen. It's about feeling misunderstood and learning that you can survive it, and, more importantly, that you can still like yourself through it.

On my own journey with rejection therapy, daring to take off the mask required a few 'tools' along the way – things that allowed me to feel grounded, things that calm down my nervous system, and habits that remind me of who I am and why I'm doing this. The first are affirmations that can help shift your core beliefs about yourself, so that when that rejection inevitably comes, you can notice it, observe it, and let it go.

Here are ten affirmations for when you begin your journey. Read them through daily, say them aloud, write your favourite ones on a Post-it note and stick them on your desk, your fridge, your bathroom mirror. Repeat them over and over again during your morning shower, or mentally repeat them on your commute – whatever it is that works for you. Try to notice the slow and subtle differences that occur when you rewire your mind with positive thinking. You might think you're mindlessly repeating statements, but you're actually rewiring your core beliefs about yourself with compassion.

## AFFIRMATIONS FOR REJECTION THERAPY

1 Fear is an important emotion; it is alerting me to what I'm afraid of, and once I know what I'm afraid of, I can learn more about myself. The secret to confidence is self-knowledge and self-awareness.
2 Rejection is redirection.
3 When I open myself up to new experiences, I open myself up to change, and when I open myself up to change, I open myself up to growth.
4 I can handle anything that comes my way. Rejection is never as bad as I believe it will be.
5 I am comfortable with rejection.
6 I am braver than I think.
7 I am capable.

The second 'tool' was breathing. Deep, full-belly, chest-rising-breaths that would ground me and my nervous system on the spot, regulating my emotions and reminding my mind: this isn't as bad as it seems.

When you begin to expose yourself to small acts of rejection, like asking for a discount at a coffee shop, complimenting a stranger, or sharing an opinion that might not land perfectly, you may notice the parts of you that tighten up, that want to retreat behind the mask. Remind yourself of these affirmations, take three deep, full-belly, chest-rising-breaths, and ignore the usual looping voice full of negativity, the ego trying to scare you into putting the mask back on.

*

During the process of writing this book, I wanted to speak to experts – experts on rejection, on pursuing their passions, on the brain and its response to rejection and perceived stress. I wanted to speak to people who have put down the mask and transformed their futures because of their ability to feel rejection and alchemise it into something powerful, changing their lives for the better, and one of those people I wanted to speak to was Sophie Tea.

Sophie Tea is a visual artist 'whose art is all about making women feel just a little bit nicer about themselves'. Famed for her 'Nude' era, she ensures her work carries an impactful message of inclusivity that celebrates the unique beauty of the female form. But you might also know her from her Charity Shop Fridays, a project with global reach, where Sophie visits a local charity shop, customises a piece with her art, and returns it to the shop for the same price – not only allowing her fans to purchase an original work by her at an accessible price, but also boosting sales and raising awareness for said local charity shop. Her reach and influence are worldwide, and she has a loyal fanbase for many reasons, with one of them being her open, authentic approach to being a visual artist and democratising affordable art.

I have long been an admirer of Sophie, not just for her beautiful artwork, often full of colour and fluidity, from her 'Nudes' series, to her abstract works, and her wildflower pieces. I have always wondered whether her artwork was a reflection of herself, whether that fluidity, that energy, that passion on the canvas was a mirror to the woman doing the painting, and I have been in awe of her trajectory and the cult following she's harnessed over the years, especially the Charity Shop Fridays series, which is where I first came across her. Since then, I've followed her work, and when the opportunity to share my experiences with rejection therapy came about, I knew I had to speak to Sophie about her own experiences dealing with the same fear.

**Sophie J: How does rejection show up for you in your life, and what is your relationship with rejection like?**

**Sophie Tea:** I'm rejected every moment of every day. Rejection is built into the culture of what I do by virtue of being an artist – it's so raw and confessional. You're putting your work out for people to unpick every day, so I deal with it all the time. Rejection is part of who I am and it's just part of the creative process. If you're not OK with putting yourself out there and having the opportunity to be rejected, you're not going to make progress.

When I first began painting, I put out my portfolio of work to galleries to ask if I could be represented. It was always a no – which is great, because the redirection has meant that I pushed towards being an independent artist and having a team internally, having my own shows. It's been a huge diversion, but sometimes that actually means you're aligned with who you are.

**Sophie J: Was there a pivotal moment of rejection for you – what did it mean for you?**

**Sophie Tea:** Over the years I've been able to reconcile with its true meaning. Rejection hurts every time. It feels like your pants are being pulled down. It's embarrassing. With age, the reconciliation that it's for the best means I'm able to sit with that and be at peace with it. In the moment, it definitely feels uncomfortable but, actually, nothing brilliant ever happens inside your comfort zone.

**Sophie J: You're on a different path to some of your artist peers – what does that feel like?**
**Sophie Tea:** Even to this day I still feel like I have an innate need, an innate desire to be accepted by the art establishment, but what I've come to realise is artists of their generation, maybe in their time, are not actually accepted. Being a social-media artist, there are negative connotations that come with it (owning your own career and selling to your own customer base). For a long time, being an Instagram artist has been looked down on, but when you look back on artists historically who have not been accepted by establishments, the entire time they're doing something that's not considered art. Isn't art about connecting with as many people as possible? Isn't the definition of art in our age, therefore, connecting on social media? That's the vehicle we can use to communicate with people now. At times I've questioned: am I actually a good artist or am I just good at creating viral videos? But communicating with so many people and being able to communicate a story to the masses, that's fine with me. I've come full circle with the idea that my time will come, so long as I keep going and continue making work that I'm proud of.

**Sophie J: In this book, I talk about the importance of affirmations and positive self-talk for dealing with rejection, as well as physical practices, like breathwork and movement. You mentioned having processes in place to protect you from yourself – what are these?**

**Sophie Tea:** Every week, whether I post it or not, I make time for what I call 'Bad Art Sundays'. I'm not painting for anyone; it's not commissioned work; it's not anything I've got to do that week that I'm finishing off; it's not something I think is going to sell – it's just crap; it's the random shit that comes out of my head, and being committed to that allows me to get back to what makes me happy and authentically me. Having that ritual in a creative life, where no two days are the same, helps. Having some stability that helps you come back to why you started – which is for the love of art – is important. It's a meditative process to be alone and paint, and that's very grounding for me. It allows me to stay authentic.

Another thing is giving myself permission to not feel guilty for how much I love my work. There are so many things online about making sure you have 'time for you', but as an artist who shares everything and is so passionate about what I do, it all brings me such joy; it challenges me; I have great relationships because of it, so I'm trying to practise not feeling bad about the fact that I'm fully immersed in my work.

**Sophie J: There's an overarching theme here – it sounds like the love you have for your work drives you through rejection. Is that the case?**
**Sophie Tea:** My work has always had my back. Even if I'm rejected, I like the fact I've built an entire world around my work. Even if I face rejection at certain points, I've still got my ability to paint; I can still add value. Rejection, and experiencing it, allows you to lean upon your own power.

After speaking with Sophie, I felt energised. This is exactly what rejection therapy is for; this is what it can help you with. Confidence, self-acceptance, empowerment. Earlier in this chapter, I talked about the importance of affirmations and breathing, how reassuring those two practices can be, but now I'd like to introduce one final practice for you to try.

## MY WEEKLY RITUAL

This ritual can be anything, anything at all, and the only rule is to do it alone. Often when it comes to checking in with ourselves, it can be easy to bury that beneath checking in with others, prioritising the needs of friends, partners, colleagues, even pets, again and again, so that between the time you wake up and the time your head hits the same pillow at night, you've made no time for yourself, and this always does more harm than good.

My weekly ritual is one ritual just for you, something that you can do once a week, every week, for as long as your rejection therapy journey lasts, and maybe it will even be something you continue to do long after your first thirty days. It can be a solo coffee date once a week at your favourite café, a cinema trip alone with just you and a bag of popcorn, a solo stroll around your favourite gallery, a quiet afternoon journalling or drawing or crafting. It can even be something more practical: a couple of hours dedicated to cleaning your space, resetting for the week, introducing a minor detour on your regular food shop to go to that bookshop round the corner to spend time browsing. The point is, it's the same thing every week, no matter what, just like Sophie Tea's Bad Art Sundays. It's a day, or a morning, an afternoon, an evening, maybe even an hour, just for you. The repetition is what makes it a ritual, the showing up is what makes it worth it.

Whatever you choose, it will be a reminder each week of the time you've carved out for yourself, and it will be the chance for you to check in on how you are doing, how your week of rejection therapy has been, and maybe, just maybe, you'll start to feel the power of your weekly ritual.

# 7

# Rethinking Rejection

I've got a secret to share here – and it might be one that surprises you. The fear within rejection therapy never fully goes away. For me, the anxiety that comes before doing a challenge has never, truly, entirely disappeared. It's always there, even if subtle. This might sound a little contradictory, especially given I'm sharing all these 'life-changing' tools and hacks to do rejection therapy, but it's true – and I'm all about honesty.

For me, the secret is learning how to handle those pre-rejection therapy challenges *before* you go into them. It's about developing your skill set so you can handle that anxiety, both before and after doing rejection therapy. This is invaluable, because you can then take those same skills and apply them to every part of your everyday life.

Now, I don't want to lose you – especially since you're seven chapters in, so don't worry about feeling the jitters. And it's worth remembering that you become a bit desensitised to the initial awkward nerves once you start the challenge, so you won't feel the anxiety as much as you might imagine. The emotions will always be there (I still feel nervous after two years of doing rejection therapy challenges) but you won't find yourself stewing on them, or the situation, for as long. We're only human, after all, and the unknown is scary. Our body and mind work to keep us safe, so going into an unknown situation with a stranger, knowing you might be rejected, will spike your nervous system. The main reason you won't fully overcome the nerves of doing rejection therapy is because your comfort zone is going to carry on growing.

However, if rejection never fully stops feeling uncomfortable, there is a bigger question to ask here: *why are we taught to experience it as failure in the first place?*

I spoke to Ben Hurst, an educator, activist and speaker who heads up Beyond Equality, a UK-based organisation that engages men and boys in the gender equality conversation, and promotes healthy masculinity and relationships. I asked him why he thinks we perceive rejection to be failing, and how we can work to shift the narrative.

**Sophie: In our society, rejection is often framed as failure. How do you show that facing rejection can be an act of strength instead?**

**Ben:** In my work, there's been a popular narrative recently about reframing rejection or failure as an opportunity for future success, and I think that has merit. But I also think there's something in our society that needs adjusting around just accepting rejection as rejection.

Sometimes there's almost a rejection of rejection, which feels rooted in a desire to control rather than accept. It's about emotional resilience – being able to take rejection without it becoming indicative of who you are as a person or meaning you're a failure. You don't have to internalise it or make it personal. You can learn from rejection, figure out what might need to change, without glossing it over or forcing a positive spin.

Sometimes you've just got lemons, and that's OK. A lot of it is about exploring the internal emotional world linked to rejection rather than reframing it as something positive. What does it feel like to be embarrassed, humiliated, sad? What does it look like to grieve a loss? These are normal parts of the human experience and don't need to be avoided. They're uncomfortable, but they're made easier in community – sitting with others, laughing, crying, or just processing together instead of pushing it aside and moving on.

**Sophie: That's such a good point. Rejection can sometimes carry social consequences, like losing**

**friends, status, or being a part of something. How do you prepare people for the impact of rejection?**

**Ben:** We live in a society where people expect results overnight – quick solutions, easy processes, step one, step two, step three, done. But sometimes living with the reality of the impact that's been caused, or the consequences of the behaviour that led to rejection, is something we have to learn to sit with. We often rush to get to the good part, to being 'over it', but there's learning and growth in those uncomfortable moments.

If you're rejected from a group, it can be useful to reflect on what happened – why people might be responding that way, and how you feel about it. Was it aligned with who you are or who you want to be? Those moments are often where the deepest change happens. When you push through too quickly, you repeat the same patterns.

Rejection can be painful and long-winded. Finding people who will sit with you through it matters, as does grappling with parts of yourself you try to avoid. It's not about fixing those parts; it's about understanding and making peace with them.

**Sophie: When we step away from a world view or group that once gave us identity or belonging, there's often an internal void. How do we survive, and thrive, in that space?**

**Ben:** The lens you view struggle, isolation or loneliness through matters. One helpful way of seeing that void is recognising that when one door closes, another can open. There's always the possibility of new connections and new communities. Seeing yourself as a multifaceted person matters. We might see ourselves as a finished product, as if who we are now is who we'll always be, but we're constantly changing. That makes these moments an opportunity to lean into different versions of yourself: find a new hobby, go and see who you might meet at a concert. I don't want to skirt over the fact that it's petrifying to feel like you're isolated or alone, but I think growth comes with thinking something different and viewing the world in a different way. Try something different, lean into a different opportunity and discover your tribe bit by bit, piece by piece.

Ben's point – that rejection can be reframed as a doorway to something new – is such a useful mindset trick. It's one I learned along the way but wish I had at the start of my rejection therapy journey. I also spoke to Ben about how we navigate fear, how it can keep us trapped, and what we can do to overcome it.

**Sophie: What role does fear play in keeping people attached to harmful identities or belief systems? How**

**do you help someone to overcome this and choose differently?**

**Ben:** I think fear is the biggest factor that keeps people in the same place, and overcoming it is so difficult. The thing I've learned is that it's usually a permission-giving exercise. When people see different options or ways of being, they feel more emboldened to try them.

If you're completely isolated – for example, the only queer person you know in your area – you can feel completely isolated in that way of being. That's why people often move to more cosmopolitan places, see others expressing themselves freely, and suddenly feel permission to be who they are. You can't give that permission to everyone, but the best thing any of us can do is be the most authentic version of ourselves that we have access to, and that will often give the people around us permission to be authentic versions of themselves.

For people who are scared of leaving or exiting those ideas of themselves, the identities they hold on to and belief systems, broadening your perspective is important – going out into the world and realising there are lots of options for who you can be and how you can be. There's also something beautiful about taking that version of yourself back to people who've always known you. They get to meet someone new, and that can become a permission-giving moment for them too.

Finding your tribe, trying different things, and meeting new people requires bravery. I remember wearing pearls for the first time and how much that was commented on – how some people were shocked by the idea of a man wearing pearls. These things are so minor that I think when people react, it's usually because it speaks to something in them that they weren't allowed to express, be, or feel like. I try not to take it too personally. Often, it's not about you; it doesn't have to stop you from being who you are – and it shouldn't.

**Sophie: If you could reframe rejection for someone who's scared of it, how would you describe it?**
**Ben:** I'd say it's really scary. You're not imagining it. You're not making it up. But you don't know that it's happened yet, and it might not be what you think it's going to be. It is an unavoidable part of life, so the quicker you can get comfortable with it, the better your life will be, in my opinion.

There's a tech-bro, Silicon-Valley way of viewing it – 'I fail one hundred times a day and every failure makes me better.' For some people that might be true – but not in my experience. But I do think the quicker we can learn to experience rejection and keep it moving, while also sitting with the emotion and taking what we need from the experience, the better we'll navigate the world. It's a constant. It happens all the time.

> You're going to experience rejection. There's no avoiding it. There's no way to get away from it. It doesn't make it less scary. But I think it's like a monster you can become friends with. Like in *Monsters, Inc.* – Boo and Sully and Mike – becoming friends with the monsters. You realise they are monsters, that part isn't a lie, but it's not necessarily what you think it is. You can have a different relationship to it. **You can be friends with rejection, rather than it always petrifying you.**

That idea of changing your relationship with rejection really stuck with me. I love the idea of seeing it as a friend. The truth is, rejection doesn't disappear, and neither does the fear, but your relationship with it can change. It's why I find affirmations such an important tool. One thing I often ask myself – which you'll find throughout the book – is, 'Am I going to die by asking this question?' Of course, the answer is always 'no'. Just having that in the back of my mind is enough to make me feel calmer.

It's this mindset that also carried me through the entire challenge. On Day 30, I went to the park and began singing – entirely unprovoked, of course – with loads of people around me. I had to face a sea of stares. Now, you might think that is TERRIFYING (because it is), but because I'd done nearly a month of challenges – and reminded myself along the way that I couldn't, and wouldn't, die – it was easy. My comfort zone had grown with that reassurance.

It's important to note here, that even though Day 30 was easy (and easier than every day that came before that), it didn't mean I wasn't nervous. The anxiety was still there, but my tolerance had developed – and therefore, my comfort zone had too. As you embark on this challenge in the next chapter, we'll look into how you approach those first thirty days. Try to think about your emotional journey. Loop back to how you felt at the start of it. With each challenge you undertake, you'll realise just how much your confidence has grown.

Like Ben said, become friends with rejection. Sit with those feelings and feel those nerves. That nervous energy *actually* matters. It's what's going to build your confidence: sitting in discomfort and realising nothing that bad can happen to you. Sure, you might feel a bit shaky or silly in the moment, but in the grand scheme of things, it really isn't that deep. What feels like a huge moment to you is often a fleeting moment for somebody else.

Let's say you walk into a shop and ask the person behind the counter if they have a spare charger. Now, in your head, that might sound really awkward. Maybe you think you're being a nuisance or simply asking for too much. They won't see it the same way. They see dozens – sometimes hundreds – of people a day, and most requests blur together.

Let's say you go into a café and ask to make your own coffee. Maybe you even decide to order a drink and then throw in a spontaneous dance when you collect it, as a challenge. In this moment, it might feel huge to you. But to that other person, it'll likely be a brief, forgettable interaction before they move on to the next customer, or simply go about their day. This raises another interesting question about rejection and where the real resistance comes from.

**Sophie: In your experience, what have you identified as the hardest thing for people to reject today: external expectations or internal narratives? Which one tends to surface first?**

**Ben:** Internal narratives are always going to surface first, but I think the difficulty is that lots of us don't recognise it when it's surfacing. I watch a lot of *Drag Race*, and RuPaul talks about inner saboteurs, and I think that's a big thing – the version of yourself inside your head that is judging you before anybody else has even had the opportunity to do so, forming beliefs about what the world's going to be like and how people are going to treat you before you've experienced it.

That chess game you're playing in your own head with yourself is probably the biggest limiting characteristic for any individual. Not to take power away from external expectations – because for lots

> of us, as children and into adulthood, who we are is shaped by those expectations – but I don't think any of them are ever more powerful than the expectations we hold about ourselves. Undoing those things is one of the hardest but most worthwhile things to do.
>
> I used to have a massive narrative about myself that I was lazy. Because I'm neurodivergent and don't work in traditional ways, I'd say all the time, 'I'm super-lazy.' My therapist kept pointing out how I'd always say this until I realised it wasn't true. That narrative shaped how I expected people to read me in every room. I didn't have to do anything except flip the switch in my head, and it completely changed how I experienced spaces – imposter syndrome disappeared because I realised I did deserve to be there.

Ben couldn't be more right here. I agree wholeheartedly that most of the time, it isn't about what other people think, and it's often all to do with us and our internal narratives. Now, I say this with love, but it's true: humans are inherently selfish. We crave connection and we have empathy for others, but at our core, we're egotistical creatures – and we always come back to thinking about ourselves. It's no surprise that we end up so in our own heads as a result!

Here's an example. Let's say you walk past a busker performing on the street. Imagine they're singing one of your favourite songs. If you were alone, you might subtly sing along, or do a little jig – likely without thinking too much about it. But let's say you're in public, or the street is really busy and you're visible. Now you might hold back. Maybe you'd smile as you pass by, thinking, 'I love this song,' but you'd likely still keep walking. The reason you wouldn't dance or sing along is simple: you're worried about being judged by the people around you.

Now, try and think about this from the busker's perspective instead. Let's say it's the first time they've ever performed on the street. Maybe they woke up nervous that morning, having thought about the performance for weeks. Maybe they'd *finally* built up the courage to set down their speaker, pick up their mic, and start singing. Maybe, for them, standing there in the middle of the street, *they* feel like everyone is staring at them – in a way, they are.

Now, what that busker would probably love *most* is that interaction – for someone to dance and sing along. To them, that wouldn't seem strange at all. After all, they're singing in public and performing for everyone to hear. Yet the person walking past might still not dance, because *they're* thinking about how they might be judged.

It's a perfect example of how most of the time we're focused completely on ourselves. You could be that person: self-conscious because you think people are watching you. Meanwhile, the busker could feel all eyes are on *them* because they're the one performing. Ironically, neither of you is really thinking about the other in the way you imagine. And that's the point – what might feel like a huge moment to you can be a passing one to another.

This realisation can be so freeing. So much of that hesitation that we feel in moments like this comes from a place of 'imagined judgement', rather than actual reality. When you start to see that people are way more focused on themselves than on you, it opens up a bigger question: what would your life look like if that fear didn't exist at all? It's something I asked Ben for his insights on – and got a pretty interesting answer!

**Sophie: If the fear of rejection disappeared tomorrow, what kind of lives do you think people would allow themselves to live? And what can we take from this?**

**Ben:** If we got rid of the fear of rejection completely, people would live more recklessly, and it could be dangerous. Sometimes the fear of rejection is a way of building in safety mechanisms, slowing us down and stopping us from doing things impulsively.

There are social scripts that exist, ways people are expected to behave around each other, and, depending on where you live, there are etiquettes that probably shouldn't just be thrown out for the sake of

> it. At the same time, people can be a lot freer when they learn to identify that fear and grapple with it, maybe wrestle it into submission or become friends with it. It gives you a lot more freedom to be who you are and do what you want. I think the quicker you can become friends with the fear and learn to manage it, the better your quality of life will be, especially the life you live inside your own head.

Ben's perspective is spot on. Yes, there are moments when social scripts exist for a reason and we do need them to live well with each other. But we can also find freedom when we're not so scared of being rejected.

Let's return to the busker story. Let's imagine you decided not to hold back when you saw them performing and you danced to the song, or sang along, instead. Imagine you weren't so worried about who might be watching and, instead, simply enjoyed the music. That small moment might have instantly lifted that busker's spirit because they could see you genuinely enjoying their performance.

And that would have ripple effects. Someone dancing in the street is random and unexpected, and that joy often happens to be contagious. Who doesn't love watching another person having a good time, letting their hair down, seeming free?

Maybe that would inspire others around you to smile, slow down – or even join in themselves.

There's something uplifting in not overthinking it. It's almost like a permission slip for everyone else to have fun too!

And often it just takes that one brave person to go first.

Stepping out and doing something different takes courage, but it's those moments where the real learning happens – including when we fail. My last question to Ben was about what rejection can teach us in these instances.

> **Sophie: Do you think there's something that rejection teaches you that success never could?**
> **Ben:** I think rejection teaches you that feeling of failure, and you can't learn that from succeeding. You can't learn what it feels like not to do well, not to meet the target, or not to achieve the goal by always achieving the goal. I don't think the takeaway is 'I'm never going to fail again'; the learning that matters is compassion and empathy for other people who experience that same thing.
>
> I work in a lot of sports academies, and you see it in some of the kids in under-eighteens' pro teams – they're so used to succeeding that they can't understand the experience of people who aren't successful. When you're eighteen years old, that might be fine, but as you grow older and start to

> experience the real world, you meet people with very different backgrounds and experiences. Some have had a tough go of it; some were dealt bad cards; some have completely messed things up.
>
> The ability to empathise, to show compassion and care, only comes from having experienced rejection or failure yourself. That's why it's important. It's a very human experience. One thing that's been normalised recently is this constant pursuit of self-improvement and becoming the perfect person who gets everything right every time, which all of us know isn't possible. No one can win all the time. Losing is OK, and you only learn that by losing. It might be painful and upsetting, but rejection teaches you how to treat people when they lose, how to treat people when you win, and how to exist well in a world with other people.

I couldn't have put it better myself. I hope Ben's insights – and that hypothetical busker story – give you the courage to be brave, to get up and dance first, to be the one who shepherds others and inspires them to enjoy themselves too.

We're not put on this planet to live small, or to not enjoy ourselves. There's no point overthinking about things like singing along with a busker, or dressing up in silly outfits, or signing up to something new. It's so easy for us to get in our heads, when, really, we can reframe and rethink how we view rejection. Rejection can make us and others, ultimately, happy, but only if we let it in.

Now we've got this mindset locked down, it's time to start our thirty days of the rejection cure!

# 8

## The First Thirty Days

Now you understand what rejection therapy is as a concept, you're going to structure a thirty-day challenge. This will help you understand how you can make rejection a part of your everyday life, how to use it efficiently, and how to get the best results in the process.

You may be feeling inspired to give rejection therapy a go, but you might also feel nervous or have some scepticism about how it can help you. All of these feelings are normal. Wherever you're at, I encourage you to trial some examples of rejection therapy. There's no pressure to complete a thirty-day challenge, and you don't need to do this to experience the benefits. Simply participating in one or two of these challenges, or a few challenges a week, will give you an opportunity to step in to that feeling of discomfort. A thirty-day challenge is particularly recommended because brain science supports it. Thirty days gives your brain plenty of time to learn that rejection can't hurt you. By the end of the challenge, having consistently experienced rejection will leave you feeling confident, empowered and far less afraid of putting yourself out there.

Let me create no illusions here – I personally found my thirty-day challenge hard, especially at the start. However, I can confidently say doing those thirty days of daily rejection therapy changed my life in ways I could never have imagined. To suddenly gain this new, unbreakable confidence and self-belief was liberating. I started to see the world, myself and people in a whole new light. For the first time in my life, I felt free. Equipped with the tools to handle rejection, put myself out there more and express myself more authentically, I stopped taking everything personally. I didn't feel defined by judgements or what other people thought of me; I realised I was so much braver and capable than I ever thought – it was, frankly, life-changing.

When I went to the park and tried to film myself doing a dance I physically couldn't do it due to the fear of being judged. It caused me to stumble on the concept of rejection therapy while scrolling online and decided to embark on the challenge. I was *so* nervous. The thought of it made my skin crawl, and I procrastinated starting the challenge for three days after posting my initial video about starting a series. I had people in my comments asking, 'Where's this challenge?' and honestly, if it wasn't for those comments, I probably wouldn't have started it.

It was terrifying – asking people ridiculous questions felt so outside the norm to me. I knew I'd be judged. 'Why would I willingly put myself in that situation?' I thought. But I reflected on it and listened to that gut feeling that told me, *Just go for it. Start small and go for it.* At this point I'd already started trying out rejection therapy in safe settings, like with my family. This helped me get used to hearing 'no'. However, I knew locking in and doing a thirty-day challenge was taking it a step further; it was about making a serious commitment.

Filming the challenge and sharing it on TikTok helped me stay accountable. For me, posting online to an audience encouraged me to carry on because I didn't want to publicly 'fail'. There was also something about people tuning in every day to watch that made me not want to let them down. The numbers weren't important. When I started, I only had around 4,000 followers. It wasn't about the social media likes or potential for virality; I was simply documenting it to hold myself to account and to hopefully inspire those watching. I had no clue, back then, what the response would be.

I have to stress, having some level of accountability is necessary to go through this challenge (unless you are seriously self-motivated and find the thrill of a challenge motivating enough). Don't underestimate thirty days of daily rejection therapy. As much as the time period doesn't seem *that* long, it can be hard to push through, at the start especially. By the time you're at day eighteen, fatigue might set in. You might find you simply can't be bothered and the last thing you feel like doing is purposely getting rejected. Motivation is naturally going to dip, so you need something to hold you accountable and keep you committed to those thirty days.

Overall, the challenge does get easier and it will change your life in ways you can't even imagine, so while it's a period of potential discomfort, try to think of it as building to a lifetime of learning that you can do hard things and that you are so much braver than you think.

### 100 Days of Rejection Therapy

Public speaker and rejection therapy advocate Jia Jiang came up with the concept of '100 Days of Rejection Therapy' (you can check out his TED Talk online), and if you want to do that, then I suggest going for it. I recommend thirty days because it's what I did, and for me, a hundred days didn't seem necessary (in fact, that felt initially quite extreme to me as a beginner!). Thirty days is a happy compromise. One month of rejection – bring it on!

## ACCOUNTABILITY PARTNERS: YES OR NO?

You might want to tell your friends, family, partner or someone you trust that you're doing rejection therapy to hold you accountable, but it's worth having a think before deciding whether to do this. Personally, I don't think an accountability partner is one of the best options, because when I told my friends that I was doing rejection therapy, I felt overwhelming judgement rather than encouragement.

My survival instinct kicked in and I felt myself wanting to justify what I was doing, why I was doing it, and asking them if they'd still like me while I was doing it, because it felt so out of my comfort zone. And this issue might not just be internal: your friends, family or partner may not understand what rejection therapy is and could, even if they're well meaning, plant a seed of doubt in your mind. Before you embark on this challenge, it's likely you'll already be feeling doubtful. So, if you do feel this inner urge to try rejection therapy and feel you'd really benefit from it – especially being able to express yourself authentically and confidently – consider keeping the challenge to yourself.

If it's the case that you feel someone in your life would be supportive and on board with what you're doing, then go for it. However, if you are unsure how they'll react, and think that their response could influence you or throw you off track, try going it alone – with the help of this book as your accountability partner instead! By the end of the thirty days, you'll feel like you've unlocked an entire new version of yourself.

A productive way to keep yourself accountable is by putting a start and end date in your calendar. Day 1 of rejection therapy might be on 1 September and then 30 September marks the end of the challenge. This gives your brain a visual, and allows you to more clearly envision the next thirty days – as well as how you can slowly build this up (one rejection a day). Having this clarity will also help you emotionally, rather than throwing your nervous system into an anxious spiral (that's not beneficial to anybody!).

## ACCOUNTABILITY TIPS

1. **Reward system**
   Treat yourself after completing a task. No matter how big or small it is. I used to not allow myself to play my favourite song until after I'd done my challenge – this really helped to motivate me. Your reward might be similar, or you might opt to do something entirely different. Whether it's treating yourself to a

nice coffee or your favourite snack, having a reward in sight will really help your mind to see past the anxiety of the challenge and remind you that there is light at the end of the tunnel.

2 **Motivational reminders**
Change your phone wallpaper to something motivational to remind you why you are doing this and to help you stay on track. You can also do the same by setting a regular alert on your phone. It could be anything that motivates you or where the language feels positive. It could simply be: *time for some fun*. These simple encouragements will propel you forward during the challenge and offer a little dopamine hit.

3 **Post yourself doing it on your social media!**
The joy of social media is that you can quickly create a community and momentum around events. People love to buy into challenges, and even if it's just your friends watching, they will likely cheer you on and be eager to watch your transformation. Not letting your audience down can be a big motivator, too. If you do post your thirty-day rejection therapy online, use the hashtag **#rejectioncure**, as I would LOVE to watch and can cheer you on in the comments.

**4 Use an accountability tracker**

You can also use an accountability tracker. Try ticking off when you've done a challenge each day. When you start getting a few ticks, the satisfaction will start to kick in and you will feel motivated to get to the end.

With all these accountability hacks, you might have decided that doing this challenge is scary or daunting, but the reality is that it really isn't. If we break down logically what you are doing for the next thirty days, it's good to remember these four nuggets of wisdom.

- **Rejection therapy is simply asking someone a question**

How many questions do you ask on a daily basis? On a weekly basis? Probably hundreds. Even if you don't ask them, you're probably thinking about them. Questions are a normal, everyday occurrence, so think of rejection therapy as simply asking someone a question.

Remind yourself that this is a quick process and it doesn't take much time out of your day. It may take five seconds, or twenty seconds, or if the person stops and you end up having a conversation, then maybe it'll take a couple of minutes. If you're caught off-guard and they end up saying 'yes' to your request, at most you might spend around twenty interacting with someone.

One time I asked to make my own coffee in a coffee shop, expecting they'd say 'no'. Instead, they said 'yes'. It was fun, the staff were really nice, and I spent twenty minutes having a new, cool opportunity. So even those twenty minutes were a win!

- **Just because someone says 'yes' doesn't mean you have to go ahead**

If someone ever says yes to your request and you don't feel comfortable, tell them what you're up to. Never feel pressured to do anything you don't want to.

Early on in my rejection therapy journey, I asked a girl in the supermarket to swap shoes with me, expecting a 'no'. Like the coffee-shop experience, I, again, got a surprising 'yes'. However, in this instance, rather than seeing this as a win, I felt a rush of panic. I didn't feel comfortable swapping shoes with a stranger so I 'broke character' and told her I was doing rejection therapy. We giggled and carried on with our days.

It's still good to be open to new experiences. In doing so, you'll have more fun. Doing rejection therapy has restored my faith in humanity because of the number of people that have said 'yes' to me unexpectedly and then I've had a fun experience and wholesome interaction.

- **See each rejection as a new – and neutral – experience**
  Getting rejected is neither good nor bad; it is just an experience. Someone pulling a face at you is neither good nor bad; it is just an experience. Someone being appreciative or giggling over your request is neither good nor bad; again, it's just an experience.

  We're conditioned to put labels on experiences, and the society we live in labels rejection as bad or negative. But rejection isn't inherently bad, and getting rejected from something could be the best thing that ever happened to you – maybe you just don't know it yet.

  Rejection could simply be redirection to something that's more aligned to your values. By telling your crush you fancy them and they don't like you back, yes, that may feel bad in the moment, but the benefit of this is that it builds your courage and confidence so you can tell the next person that you fancy them – and that person could just be the love of your life. Of course, rejection doesn't always feel nice, and we are allowed to feel disappointment, but a lot of its power comes from the unnecessary fear and meanings we've placed on it. **Rejection**

**is often painted as something to avoid at all costs or something that's terrible, but it doesn't have to be.**

- **Reframe rejection as an opportunity to realign** Let's say you got rejected from a job you *thought* you wanted, and that allowed you to actually end up getting the job of your dreams. Trust everything is always working out perfectly and getting rejected is simply redirection to your more aligned path.

*

## TACKLING DAY 1

Day 1 is likely to be the hardest, because your brain hasn't experienced getting rejected in a controlled way before. The fear of the unknown might completely take over, and your mind may throw a million and one reasons – and excuses – at you to NOT do the challenge.

This reaction isn't just exclusive to the first day of the challenge and can crop up any time during the thirty days. What's crucial is that you maintain a clear mindset and remind yourself that when this resistance kicks in, you shouldn't see it as a sign to stop.

When I started, I experienced this anxiety for nearly two weeks, but I didn't have the right tools to help me. Some days my anxiety was so high that

I questioned why I was even doing the challenge. I often found myself thinking, 'Why am I putting myself through this?' Now, looking back, I'm so glad I kept going.

My advice to you? When all these excuses flood in, remind yourself that this is your brain trying to protect you. In moments like this, say *thank you* to it. Your brain is designed to keep you safe, and rejection is one of those things that our brain deems as life-threatening (even if, logically, we know it's not). As you are stepping out of your comfort zone, your brain triggers the safety-alarm bells and will try to stop you. It will start feeding you excuses (that seem believable), telling you why you shouldn't do what you're doing, which, in this case, is the challenge.

When your brain is telling you things like, 'I don't want to be annoying', 'I don't want to bother them', or 'I'm not pretty enough', all that's happening is that it's stepping into the unknown. This is scary for the brain. It likes to control situations and predict outcomes for the sole purpose of keeping us safe. So when embarking on your rejection therapy challenge, your 'Day 1' mind is likely to give you a million reasons *not* to do it. 'What if they are rude to me? What if I get kicked out?' These thoughts can be loud and, in some cases, you might start believing them. That's OK – it means your brain is doing its job correctly. However, what is important to remember is that these are not facts. The goal isn't to push away these thoughts but to change our relationship with them. Where a lot of us go wrong in everyday life is believing that every thought we have is a fact. If we hear any negativity, we stop in our tracks and think, 'Oh, it must be true' (even when it's not!).

We can allow these thoughts in, but the key is to not let them win. A huge part of rejection therapy is overcoming the limitations of your mind. When your mind is giving you excuses not to do a rejection therapy challenge, it's the same as when you want to reach out to an old friend, but you don't want to 'bother them'. Or when your coffee order comes out wrong and you don't want to be 'annoying' by taking it back.

By practising hearing the limitations in rejection therapy, and saying, 'Thank you, brain, for trying to protect me, but I'm going to be fine', before doing said challenge, you begin to see the truth: your thoughts are, indeed, not facts. The outcome will rarely be as bad as you expected, and your confidence will improve. Cue the #feelingproud of yourself.

### *And in Worst-case Scenarios?*

Let's say a worst-case scenario happened and someone was rude to you. This isn't as terrible as you think, because it proves to your brain that, even when faced with the worst outcome, **you can handle it.** You survived; you're still breathing. Yes, it may have felt slightly uncomfortable and awkward in the moment, but it's just that: a moment. Outside of this, what changes?

The most powerful thing you can do in this scenario is show your brain you can handle discomfort. When you repeatedly prove to your brain that no matter the funny look you received, judgement you felt, or abrupt 'no' you got, you're still fine, your resilience builds.

**Five things you can tell yourself when you've experienced pushback**

1. **The world won't stop spinning**
   As I've mentioned above, even in the worst-case scenarios, you will still walk away breathing. You'll still be the same person – you won't be defined by an interaction. Reminding yourself that this is simply an experience (neither good or bad) and you can choose how to respond to it will help to ground you.
2. **I am not going to die by doing this challenge**
   You will not die by slowly pushing yourself out of your comfort zone even though it might feel like it. When you're feeling the nerves, your hands are shaking and sweaty, and you

feel hot, you might think otherwise, but early on in your rejection therapy journey your brain hasn't learned that yet (hence why day one can feel the hardest).

3 **Anticipation is always worse than action**
Anxiety will always cripple you before a challenge, and lead you to put it off. The longer you sit in that anticipation, the harder the challenge will become. Again, this is no fault of our own; this is our brain's survival mechanism kicking in. Your best way of overcoming this is simple: go out and DO it.

### Fight, flight or freeze

The amygdala is the area in the brain responsible for fear. This detects threats and danger, and responds in one of three ways: fight, flight or freeze. When you do something unfamiliar or scary, the amygdala takes control. It floods you with nervousness, fear, and convincing excuses designed to stop you from taking action. Not because you're in danger – but because your brain is wired to avoid discomfort. The key is learning to recognise when your amygdala is reacting to perceived fear, not real threat, and choosing to move forward anyway.

4 **Don't think, just do**
This saying has carried me through rejection therapy. As someone who does this daily, even I am not immune to sometimes falling victim to the old amygdala response, which can make me anxious, make my heart race, or make me procrastinate doing a challenge. This is where not thinking and just doing is vital – not giving yourself the time to build up a challenge in your head, just to get nervous and put it off for most of the day.

5 **It's never as bad as you think**
It's only by '**feeling the fear and doing it anyway**' that your brain gets evidence that what you are doing can't physically hurt you. Realising that getting rejected, getting judged and being perceived can't touch you, and therefore understanding that it's never going to be as bad as you think, will help you on your journey.

*Becoming desensitised to rejection*

Repeated exposure to rejection – with the correct tools to manage it – will create a desensitised response. Eventually, rejection therapy will feel like an exciting adrenaline sport. You might begin to feel invincible, purposely seeking out ways to get that buzz and thrill.

When your brain learns that the word 'no' really doesn't have an impact on you or your day, you'll understand that someone can't hurt you, unless you give them permission to. This is the magic of rejection therapy. It's uncomfortable at the start, but if you can continue to push through, it allows your brain to reprogramme and learn that rejection isn't dangerous.

And how does that positively impact your life?

It means you can show up at work and contribute ideas and thoughts in forums without a second thought, because YOU know it doesn't matter what your colleagues think or say about those ideas – or you. It means you can go to the gym and not feel bothered about how people look at you, or how they might perceive you. It means that if a friend doesn't want to meet up, you don't see it as a personal attack or a judgement on your character. Instead, you'll show up with an inner confidence, control and sense of freedom – because you've taught your brain that no matter what others think, say or do, it doesn't define YOU.

## WHAT DO I DO, POST-CHALLENGE?

It's important to know how to deal with the aftermath of doing a rejection therapy challenge. You might feel nervous, shaky or embarrassed. This is normal, and it's because it's so new and unfamiliar to the brain that it's impacting your nervous system. Your adrenaline is likely to be high and it's important to know how to regulate this, because the point of rejection therapy is to feel some discomfort, be able to sit with that, and learn it's not a threat and work through it. The point is to not have you feeling like an anxious mess.

*Here's how you can ground yourself after a challenge.*

BREATHING EXERCISES

This one's especially helpful if you're feeling shaky. Inhale through your nose for four seconds, hold for four, exhale for eight. There are many different breathing techniques, and the goal is to use whatever works for you, but it's important you inhale deeply through your **nose, hold** for a **moment** and then exhale. Repeat this three to five times, or until feeling calmer.

What this does is tell your nervous system, 'I am safe.' Breathing techniques activate the parasympathetic nervous system, which shifts your body out of fight or flight. After doing rejection therapy, especially at the start, your body has gone through a mini threat response, so it's important to regulate yourself. Deep breathing carried me through rejection therapy and I genuinely don't think I would have been able to do it without it so *never* underestimate the power of the breath.

## GROUNDING AFFIRMATIONS

Remind yourself you are safe. Your internal dialogue after doing rejection therapy is really important. If you walk away from a challenge thinking, 'They probably think I'm so stupid,' or, 'Why did I do that?' or, 'I'm embarrassed,' then you're going to continue to feel anxious.

Your internal dialogue after doing rejection therapy has to be empowering. It's important to channel thoughts that are productive and serve a positive outcome. Naturally, after doing a challenge, your mind might run away with a self-deprecating narrative. That is understandable (and normal!), but the key thing to remember is that if you ruminate on these disempowering thoughts, you're going to stay feeling anxious longer than needed. The goal is to try and calm your nervous system as soon as possible. Affirmations will help you to do this.

Repeat this three to five times, either aloud or in your head: 'I am safe. No one is thinking about me other than me.'

## REFLECTIONS

There's no faster way to calm any nervous energy than by reflecting. Ask yourself, 'Was that as bad as I thought?' after every rejection therapy challenge, and notice how you *really* feel.

Our brain is quick to automatically think something is embarrassing because, societally, we perceive it to be, but when we tap into how we actually feel inside, it's likely we feel something else entirely – liberated, positive, brave, empowered even! To move away from that conditioning, reflect on how you truly feel after doing a challenge.

*Note:* How you feel might change throughout the thirty-day challenge. It may depend on what challenge you did that day, but after you've done it, try to ask yourself, 'Has the world stopped spinning?' Questioning will help to ground you and drive you closer to a non-reactive emotional state.

If it was uncomfortable, sit with that discomfort. As a society, we run so far away from discomfort and seek to avoid embarrassment at all costs. Ironically, that is one of the main reasons why we don't know how to handle rejection, so see the challenge as doing the work to undo this!

### *Embarrassment is an unexplored emotion – go and make a fool of yourself*

I want to be clear about this: **please use your own discernment.** Everyone's body, nervous system, limits and capacities are different. What feels manageable for one person may feel overwhelming for another.

I'm sharing what has helped me, but you know yourself better than anyone else. Sitting with some discomfort can be healthy and allow for growth, but only you can decide when discomfort tips into too much.

**You always have the right to listen to your body, your needs and your boundaries. If something feels like too much, you don't have to do it.**

The purpose of rejection therapy is gradual exposure, building tolerance and confidence over time. Going in at full speed, without easing your nervous system into it, can be counterproductive. If your brain has never been exposed to discomfort, starting with something extreme can overwhelm rather than empower you.

**Start where you feel safe enough to stretch.** That might mean practising with friends first. It might mean low-stakes interactions with strangers. There is no correct pace.

This is meant to be a challenge that empowers you in a way that feels safe, controlled, and light-hearted. Trust yourself. Your body will tell you what it's ready for.

## GETTING STARTED

To help you get started on your rejection therapy journey, I have created a thirty-day-challenge template that you can follow.

This starts with smaller challenges and builds, so that your nervous system and brain can appropriately adjust. This is just a guide, so feel free to pick and choose certain challenges, to alter any to make them better fit with your lifestyle, to come up with your own, or even make some harder!

Use this as a rough guide: should you commit to seeking out rejection at least once a day for the next thirty days, it will transform your life and your confidence.

Let's go!

# 9

## The Thirty-Day Template

### YOUR GOAL

Purposely seek rejection every day for thirty days. Each time you hear a 'no', you prove to yourself that:

- You can handle discomfort.
- Discomfort always passes.
- You don't need external validation to feel worthy.
- Most imagined outcomes are far worse in your mind than in reality.

### YOUR SAFETY RULES

1. **Respect boundaries**
   Never pressurise or manipulate anyone. A 'no' must be safe and final.
2. **Keep it ethical**
   Don't ask for anything illegal, unethical or inappropriate.

3 **Avoid children and vulnerable people**
Never involve children or anyone who cannot safely say 'no'.
4 **Stay in public spaces**
For challenges with strangers, avoid isolated areas.
5 **Prioritise your physical safety**
Don't ask for anything that could put you in obvious danger.

**These challenges are designed to expose you to brief discomfort in a safe and controlled way, not to harm yourself or others.**

GUIDANCE

- Include an accountability tracker (for yourself).
- Keep a daily log of prompts.

**Ask yourself:**
1 How did I feel before?
2 How did I feel during the challenge?
3 How did I feel after completing it?
4 What felt easier/harder than expected

**Rate your feelings**
Keep a log of how nerve-racking you found each challenge. This is a great way to monitor your growth and see how you're doing, like the example below:

On a scale of 1–10, how nervous did I feel before doing that challenge?

1 2 3 4 5 6 7 8 9 10

Not anxious Anxious

SELF-REFLECTION QUESTIONS

- What fears or worries do I have about doing this challenge? (For example, rejection, judgement, awkwardness, embarrassment.)
- What do I believe will happen if I get rejected?
- How do I normally react to rejection or uncomfortable situations?
- What would I do differently in my life if I wasn't afraid of rejection?
- What kind of person do I want to become by the end of these thirty days?
- What is one promise I can make to myself during this challenge? (For example, I will show up even when it's uncomfortable.)

WEEK-BY-WEEK TEMPLATE

Below you'll see some examples as a guide, but feel free to tweak and adapt for your personal life and goals. There truly is an abundance of rejection therapy ideas, so feel free to alter or come up with your own where needed.

*Week 1: Starting Small*
(try these with people you know)

**Day 1**
**Ask for a small favour.**
Ask someone, maybe a friend, to help you out or do a tiny task for you.

- Borrow a pen or charger from someone.
- Ask a friend to grab a coffee or drink for you.
- Ask someone to pass you something you can't reach.

**Day 2**
**Request a skill-sharing session.**
Ask someone you know to teach you something (for example, applying make-up, drawing, a music lesson, recipe tips, public-speaking advice).

- How do you style your hair like that – could you teach me?
- How do you edit your photo like that – could you teach me?
- Could you give me some tips on confident public speaking?

- How do you make your sandwiches – could you teach me?

**Day 3**

**Ask to borrow something slightly inconvenient.**

Not money – but something mildly effortful.

- A book someone hasn't finished reading.
- A jacket.
- A kitchen tool.
- A hairbrush.

**Tip:** The goal isn't to get the item; the goal is to get comfortable asking, even when it feels slightly inconvenient.

**Day 4**

**Suggest a plan that might not suit them.**

Invite someone to an event or activity that's more your idea than theirs.

- Do you want to grab a drink together after work?
- Do you want to come to my gym class with me?
- Can we watch this film I've picked tonight? (Even better if it's an obviously bad film choice.)

**Day 5**
**Ask for honest feedback.**
On your outfit, social-media bio, CV, or a recent decision.

- Do you like my outfit?
- What do you think of my social-media profile?
- What's one thing you noticed about me when we first met?
- Is there anything I could improve on my CV?

**Tip:** The goal isn't approval; the goal is to learn that feedback is simply information and perspective – not a reflection on your identity or worth.

**Day 6**
**Ask for an introduction.**

- Would you introduce me to your friend who works in X?
- Could you introduce me to the manager? Then say something positive!
- Could you introduce me to your friends?

**Tip:** You're not asking to be chosen; you're opening a new door using connections.

**Day 7**
**Ask to join an existing plan.**

- Can I tag along to that dinner?
- Can I join you for lunch?
- Could I join that meeting? I'd love to hear what it's about.
- Could I come to a gym session with you?

**Tip:** You're not intruding; you're practising belonging and connection.

*Week 2: Branching Out*
(stepping slightly into the unknown)

Note, now you have an idea of some prompts, empower yourself to think about examples for the following weeks!

**Day 8**
**Ask a stranger for the time.**

**Day 9**
**Give a genuine compliment to a stranger.**

**Day 10**
**Ask for directions, even if you know them.**

**Day 11**
**Wave at three random cars going by.**

**Day 12**
**Ask a staff member in a shop for help even if you don't need it.**

**Day 13**
**Start a conversation with someone in an unexpected place (for example, a queue, bus stop or bench).**

**Day 14**
**Ask for a discount in a shop.**

*Week 3: Time to Be Playful and Bold*
(it's all about becoming braver)

**Day 15**
**Ask a stranger to take a photo of you.**

**Day 16**
**Ask for a small freebie (for example, a cake, a food sample).**

Day 17
Try and high-five a stranger.

Day 18
Ask an obvious question (for example, 'Does this shop sell eggs?').

Day 19
Ask someone to play 'Rock, Paper, Scissors' with you.

Day 20
Ask a stranger if they'd like to see a picture of your pet or a prized possession.

Day 21
Message a celebrity on social media asking for a follow back or shout-out.

*Week 4: Bigger Risks*
(but higher rewards)!

Day 22
Tell a joke to someone in an unexpected place (for example, to the shop cashier, in a lift, to the bus driver, to the coffee-shop worker).

Day 23
Post on your social media something you'd usually overthink (for example, a story, a selfie, a business promotion, a talking-to-camera video).

Day 24
Ask for a small rule exception (for example, asking to extend a deadline, calling up to try and get a table at a fully booked restaurant).

Tip: You're not breaking rules; you're practising asking for flexibility without fear.

Day 25
Ask to use the staff toilet in a shop or restaurant.

Day 26
Hug a tree in a public space.

Day 27
Go out in public wearing something unexpected (like your pyjamas) – nip to the shop, go for a walk, etc.

Day 28
Ask to make your 'something' yourself (for example, a coffee in a coffee shop, pizza in a pizza takeaway).

*Week 5 (or the final two days!): Ambitious Targets!*

**Day 29**
**Ask for something clearly beyond norms, for example, 'Can I get this meal for free if I wash dishes?'; (use a playful tone).**

**Day 30**
**Do a thirty-second dance in an unexpected place – in the supermarket, at the park, at work, in front of your friends (think of this as a celebration for ticking off the thirty-day challenge!).**

**You don't build confidence by avoiding the 'no'. You build confidence by facing it and proving to yourself you don't have to let it control or define you.**

## POST-CHALLENGE JOURNAL PROMPTS

- Looking back, how do I feel about rejection now compared to Day 1?
- What was the hardest part of this challenge and what did I learn from it?
- What surprised me most about people's reactions?
- What was my favourite challenge and why?

- In my daily life, where have I noticed my confidence changing the most over the last thirty days?
- What is my biggest takeaway from doing this challenge?

# 10

## Your Relationship with Rejection

The thing to remember about rejection is that it is never going to go away if you're living your life to the full. And, actually, when you think about rejection in this way – that it can only occur when you're being brave, when you're *trying*, when you're simply living, then you can take it a lot more for what it is: part of our human experience. And just like death, family conflict, growing up, all of the things that are part of our human experience, you have to learn how to live with them and what your relationship to these life occurrences and emotions are. Your relationship with rejection – the way you define it, whether you view it as a hindrance or an opportunity, whether it makes you feel like a victim or like you're simply facing another challenge – will change the way you react to it and the way you prepare for it.

Now that you've begun your thirty-day challenge of the rejection cure, I'm sure you'll begin to notice all of this a lot more. The finite timeline of thirty days gives you the opportunity to study yourself and your relationship with rejection and, maybe, a lot of other emotions that are rising to the surface.

Three things to remember while on this journey:

1 **You're going to annoy someone: Accept it.**
The idea of potentially annoying someone has massively held me back in my rejection therapy journey. What I've come to learn is: you'll never predict who may feel slightly annoyed or who who feels thrilled by your request. You could annoy one person and make the next person's day. Remember, you can't feel responsible for everybody's thoughts and feelings, and trying to predict people's reactions will only hold you back.

2 **Humans love novelty.**
Humans love experiencing something a little out of the ordinary. It stimulates our brains and breaks us out of our autopilot mode. That's why, when there's a street performer, a lot of people stand around and listen and watch. When you are doing your rejection therapy challenge, most people will not be annoyed by your harmless antics and will likely be amused. The people that *do* get annoyed were likely already annoyed in the first place – and that isn't your responsibility. What is your responsibility is to not be rude, but rejection is, ultimately, harmless fun.

3 **No one thinks about you as much as you think about yourself.**
The people that get annoyed and the people that get entertained are all going to go home and likely not think about the event again. Yes, they may occasionally bring it up to a friend if it really tickled them (because, as we've learned, humans love novelty), but, ultimately, everyone is so focused on themselves and their own lives that asking your rejection therapy question is just a passing moment to that person.

I spoke to Caroline Beaton, a comedian, keynote speaker, podcaster, awards host, business leader and bestselling author. Well known for being a natural storyteller, Cally is one of the UK's most sought-after names for corporate, broadcasting and live comedy work. I asked her what her relationship with rejection is, and why it's something we need to embrace rather than avoid.

**Sophie: Rejection is something that we can feel at any age, but for a lot of people their first experiences can be quite early on. Do you remember when you first felt rejection?**

**Cally:** I had red hair, I was overweight, I wore glasses, and my parents were both teachers at my school. So my whole childhood was pretty uncomfortable, and I think that led to what I do now.

I got bullied a lot and I always stood out, so I grew up assuming that I'd be rejected. The thing you then realise is you reject yourself at a certain point and you end up pushing yourself out into the cold instead of building a lovely relationship with yourself where you can withstand it. I'm fifty-six years old now and it's taken me most of my life to start to unpick all of that.

**Sophie: 'Rejecting yourself': I've never thought about it like that. What did that look like for you?**
**Cally:** Masking, overcompensating and trying to please people and make people think that I had all the answers. It took the form of not in any way admitting I was vulnerable or showing any chinks in the armour, let alone showing other people. I talk a lot about vulnerability as a corporate speaker, that it isn't about what you show the outside world, but what relationship you have with yourself. What am I actually feeling? Vulnerability is at the heart of that.

**Sophie Jones: Was there a turning point for you?**
**Cally:** I had spent many years in boardrooms and senior roles in television and film. I'd never done stand-up before; I did my first in my mid-forties and late forties properly as a pro, but I was used to speaking on stages for many years with a corporate

hat, where you are supposed to be glossy and look the part.

I gave a speech at a big forum for lots of personal assistants at the O2 and I was the opening speaker. I'd had a really bad bit of news and been tearful all night and turned up tear-stained and distressed. I got on stage and I said, 'I don't know how I'll get through this. I look the part, but I don't know how I'm going to give you all this speech,' but then I did a normal, good speech and after I thought, 'Why did I say that?' But the response I got in that room added to the power of it, and my vulnerability and authenticity are what stood out from that speech. That has taught me as a speaker to turn up with where I am and what's going on, rather than where I think people want me to be, and I think that invites people in.

**Sophie: You weren't feeling yourself. Was your brain giving you reasons for asking, 'Why did you say that?'**

**Cally:** Absolutely. Even during the speech, I had that voice in my head. When you're doing something public-facing there's not a lot of time for an inner critic because you're performing, but the inner critic was starting: 'Oh God, how embarrassing,' then I was like, 'Oh, right, the response from others is not shame or embarrassment.'

And this is at the heart of what you do, Sophie, and what you stand for. When you hold shame up to the light, it dissipates. Shame is an internal, scary thing that has its power when we keep its secrets, but when we hold it up to the light, it loses that power.

**Sophie: That's so true. Your mind can tell you all these stories and lie to you, but it doesn't mean it's the reality of the situation. That's a great story.**

**Cally:** Exactly, as a stand-up, what people want is the chinks in the armour. No one wants to come away thinking, 'They were so sorted.' They want to hear the mess and you have to show it. You can't just tell it; you have to show it as well as tell it, and that means showing it to yourself first. In a stand-up environment, vulnerability and mess are crucial. In corporate work, it's amazing how thousands of people who are on their best behaviour in their nice work clothes, all they want to hear is what the story is behind the story they know. If you are successful but a messy person, well, it's reassuring and relatable: 'I can still do things.'

My whole thesis now is to try things, do things, be willing to fail and do not expect the mess to go away; let it go on your journey with you and know that you're being brilliant with it taking it with you.

Cally's point, about embracing the failures and being willing to show your messy side, is such a central part of the rejection cure and a realisation I wish I'd had much earlier in this journey. However, I know how difficult it can be to embrace those uncomfortable emotions. And it's supposed to be! When the fear kicks in, when the amygdala is triggered, when your nerves creep up and the anxiety overrides you in that moment – whether on stage, or just in a room with friends – it's important to know that you have tools at your disposal that *will* help this to go away, that will help you get through that particular example and feel great on the other side of it.

I spoke to Cally about what tools she has to cope with this vulnerability.

**Sophie: When you're in the public eye and being open about being vulnerable, even with comedy, you have to show up slightly messy. What kind of coping strategies do you have to feel safe?**

**Cally:** On the corporate circuit, I find power in taking that mess with me when I'm backstage. The last thing I tell myself before I go out there is just 'be present'. It comes down to a question of not what you're going to do but how you're going to do it; the words never save you but how you turn up will. Properly trying to engage with people and how I'm presenting is going to take the heat off. I try to tell myself that I am enough, even if how I'm feeling that day is really small. It's not a 'You're amazing you can do anything,' type of inner dialogue, it's 'I'm OK, I can do it. I've had a long day but I'm OK.'

**Sophie Jones: And would you say that positive self-talk is important?**

**Cally:** Rather than positive, I'd say accepting. Accepting self-talk. Sometimes turning it into a positive is really hard. I use a gentle self-care approach: how you would parent if you were talking to a child, what you would say to them, which is what to say to yourself, and that wouldn't be, 'You'll be the best sheep in the play ever; you'll be the most amazing child out there,' it's, 'Everyone is dying to see you in your sheep outfit, and just be yourself, and just enjoy it.' That type of dialogue is kind and accepting.

**Sophie Jones: Do you think that an overemphasis on being positive can become toxic?**

**Cally:** I think it can, and that can lead to inadequacy for not feeling positive enough, which can lead to all sorts of things when, actually, if you're feeling sadness or grief, it's good to sit with that. I'll let that pass by like the clouds in the sky. And also, trust yourself; as comedians, we do it so often you'd be amazed the state we can be in and have a good show. There can be terrible traffic and you can be really ill and have food poisoning, but you can always turn up and in the moment you'll be OK.

It's a heightened thing, being on stage, the adrenaline in front of people, and having nowhere to hide, but you have to commit to the bit. Once you're up there, in those seconds or minutes when you're doing it, you're not thinking of anything other than this; there's no bandwidth left for self-doubt or an inner critic because you have to just do it.

**Sophie: So, feel the fear and do it anyway?**
**Cally: Feel the failure and do it anyway.** If you think about why people don't do things, you're asking what are you scared of? Failure. Looking stupid; thinking it'll go wrong. Well, you are going to fail; you are going to look stupid, and things will go wrong in your life at multiple points, but it's a fool's errand to try and avoid it. At the end of the day, I'll end up safe in bed; in the scheme of human existence at the moment, that's not a huge problem.

And the people who love you are just going to love you. My kids and my dogs, the things that actually matter and the human connections, they aren't affected by these things, and there's a lot of ego to how much we attribute to a bad gig and how people look at us in a bad dress, and that went wrong, and so on, when actually no one cares; no one's looking; no one's interested.

People ask me do I regret not doing this earlier, but I couldn't have done it when I was younger. I took a few knocks in life and it takes life experience for me to have this perspective. It's an interesting world with loads of rejection and I applaud the people in their twenties doing it, but I couldn't have. Years on the planet and doing loads of gigs has built the muscle memory up.

**Sophie: Do you remember your first ever gig?**
**Cally:** Like lots of people, I did an eight-week comedy course and at the end of it I did a gig in front of people in a pub. The audience is friends and family, so it couldn't be a softer, warmer room. It didn't go well. I was good on the course, knew how to use a mic and props; I understood what was comedic, but I was too buttoned up and polished, like I was reciting a script, and it didn't work brilliantly. Then I did a second and tried to do the opposite and just be loose, and it went really well. They say you're never as good as your best gig and never as bad as your worst, so I kept that in mind and have used it to keep going.

Finding what keeps you going is something that really stuck with me. Thirty days is a long time, even though it sounds like a short, easy, one-month challenge. It will come with ups and downs, off days and down days, and you'll want to have support throughout it. This is where your toolkit from Chapter 3 comes in. Go back to the intentions you set at the start of this challenge to remember why you're doing this. Go back to 'How You Want to Feel' (page 26) and remember that confidence is something you build and develop over time, and that simply by starting this challenge, you're already halfway there to changing your life.

Like Cally said, the people who love you are going to love you, so at the end of every single day of this challenge, remember that. It's OK to look and feel stupid sometimes – it's part of life! Embracing that vulnerability will be a marker for where you can grow.

**Sophie: Do you remember a moment in your career when you felt massive rejection?**

**Cally:** So many; they come thick and fast as a performer. I still don't know if I handle it well. I take it personally. I've got quite thin skin, probably thinner skin than I should have, and it does usually knock me a bit, but I have more faith in 'this too shall pass', and I notice that if it's really hard, I find going on about it makes it worse. So I focus instead on being peaceful and doing things that keep me well – walking my dog, being in nature, talking to my kids, nice restorative things.

I think it still hurts me and hits me badly, trolling and things, but I don't let it blow my skirt up as much. I keep walking and know it will unhurt again. We are hugely resilient as human beings and we will get ourselves to an OK place, even if we have no tools, and if you just know that, it's quite relaxing. I'm not going to wallow in it or fight it; I'm just going to let it play out.

**Sophie Jones: You started your podcast *Namaste Motherf*ckers* in 2021 and it's hugely popular now. Did you feel any nervousness when you started it?**
**Cally:** I did. I started it not during lockdown but after, where there was a proliferation and it might not have cut through, but we've already done over 200 episodes so far.

I don't think I've ever done one I wasn't proud of, and I've never butchered an interview, so I must be all right at it. I was relieved when I heard a clip from Marc Maron from the *WTF* podcast, which has been running for a couple thousand episodes, for nearly twenty years. He's had Obama and film stars and massive names, and they were being released two to three times a week. On his final episode, I was amazed to hear him say he gets scared every time he does an interview. That he's always anxious. I thought, 'I'm so relieved' because I get disproportionate anxiety around my podcast.

It's quite intimate, and if I manage to secure a big name it's by approaching [them] myself, and it's a lot of effort for me. If I've got Paloma Faith for an hour, I'll think, 'What if she hates me? What if I offend her?' I didn't have any fear about launching the podcast, but I did have a lot around the interview and the interviewees; it's definitely one of the harder things I do.

**Sophie: That's such a great point, especially about Marc Maron. We can always feel a little bit like we're nobody, even when we reach a certain point of success.**

**Cally:** I think it's a helpful thing. We are nobody and most people aren't successful or in the public eye for long. You'll see someone's star shine very brightly for two, three, ten years, but it's rarely very long. It's more likely we'll be inhabiting a post-famous world for longer than a famous one, and also that side of things doesn't make you happy. No amount of fame makes you happy. It gives you dopamine for a moment, but it doesn't give you fulfilment. Imagine – you can't go out and have a bad day because you're in the public eye all the time. You have to be careful what you wish for. Hopefully that's the message that will stick.

**Sophie: When did you start to get into self-help?**

**Cally:** When I wrote my book, my editor called to say, 'You've hit the *Sunday Times* bestseller list and are number one in self-help in the UK.' I said, ''Have I written a self-help book?' And she said, 'What did you think you'd written?' 'I don't know,' I said. I think I've been in an area of self-exploration forever. It was for me, more like a chat with all my girlfriends, trying to work stuff out and talk stuff through.

**Sophie Jones: OK, last question: what advice would you give to your younger self, or what advice would you have for someone stepping out of their comfort zone but feeling fearful of rejection?**

**Cally:** No one knows what they're doing; everybody thinks they're going to be found out. Instead of trying to fight that feeling, take it with you on your journey because it will be the voice that helps you get through things. That vulnerable and imposter voice will take care of you – don't try to get rid of it.

Think about what it is you're scared of and what's holding you back. If the answer is failure or it might not work, that's not a reason not to do it. There's no success without failure: all you need to do is **fail forward.** I never learn as much from a good gig as I do from a bad gig, so it's really useful if you get that feedback.

I couldn't agree with Cally more. There's so much waiting for you on the other side of the rejection cure.

Failing forward, putting yourself in uncomfortable situations, leaning into the vulnerability instead of away from it, is where you find success, joy, growth and the version of yourself you've been waiting so long to meet.

I hope Cally's insights – and her bravery to take on new challenges, seemingly at every stage of her life so far – can give you the courage to be brave, too, and to do it with kindness towards yourself above all else. It isn't just about the next thirty days, even though they're the key foundation for building this new chapter full of confidence and new opportunities. It's about how to approach each new milestone inevitably heading your way and how to feel prepared for it, and even embrace it.

# 11

## Rejection at Work

Workplace rejection can feel personal, whether it's a role you didn't land, an idea that was overlooked, an email that went unanswered, feedback that stung more than expected or even online social rejection. It tangles itself with identity, competence and self-worth and often feels more like a verdict on your whole being than rejection.

For a long time, I believed rejection at work meant I was not good enough. If I put an idea forward and it wasn't chosen, I attached that rejection to my self-worth. Instead of being able to effortlessly shrug it off or get my brain to process (logically) that it was OK for my idea not to be chosen, I saw this as a rejection of me. I felt embarrassed that I spoke up and it wasn't good enough, feeling incompetent at my role, thinking I shouldn't have brought the idea to the table in the first place. This all would happen subconsciously, within a split second, and I would feel discomfort, along with racing thoughts. All of this, just because my idea wasn't chosen.

The problem was that I'd internalised outcomes as evidence. If my workload was passed on to someone else, I would take it personally, assuming everyone had been talking badly about me behind my back. I'd compare myself to my colleagues, wondering why they could do tasks that I found hard. I'd create stories, imagining what my colleagues and manager thought of me. These stories felt convincing but were rarely true. I only felt good at my job if I was doing things 'right': if I got the nod of approval from my manager, or the dopamine hit when my idea was chosen. I was constantly seeking external validation, which is sad because I was good at my job. But my unknown insecurities were triggered at every point of rejection, no matter how big or small.

What I didn't realise back then, and I know now, is **the damage was not caused by the rejection itself, but by the meaning and narrative I attached to the rejection.** I made assumptions and created stories when I felt rejected, but, in actual fact, it was never personal. My idea not being picked didn't mean it was a bad one; it meant someone else's idea was more suitable. The workload being passed to another colleague wasn't because I was incapable of doing it myself; it was given to another person to help me out and take the pressure off. I'd attached meanings to the rejection that weren't true, and that was what was hurting me. I had this yearning to be liked, and anything that jeopardised that would be internalised, with me thinking I was bad at my job. All of this came from my own beliefs about myself and, because I wasn't yet self-aware, I couldn't then heal.

In this chapter, we're going to learn how to separate your worth from outcomes, how to respond to rejection with professionalism instead of self-punishment, and how to use rejection intentionally as a tool and not a threat.

## THE HIDDEN COST OF ASSUMING WHAT OTHERS THINK

One of the biggest traps we fall into at work is assuming we know what people think about us. We treat colleagues, managers or clients as if they are mind-readers, judging and evaluating our every move. We create stories in our minds, like: 'They probably think I'm not capable; they regret hiring me; everyone knows what they're doing except me. If I ask a question, they'll think I didn't listen; my manager is noticing every mistake I make; maybe I look like I'm trying too hard. I feel like my colleagues don't like me; I look awkward and everyone is noticing.' But the truth is...

**People are not mind-readers, but we often live as though they are.**

Notice how many times in your day, in your week, you are assuming what people think of you? How many times are you assuming what people will say or think with no evidence?

That's the key part – **no evidence.**

Just because you feel a certain way doesn't mean everybody else feels the same. Just because you're thinking something negative about yourself doesn't mean other people think it too.

**You are not a mind-reader.** By assuming you are, you end up hurting yourself unnecessarily. You create stress that doesn't need to exist, replaying conversations, analysing silence, and attaching meaning where there may be none. The truth is, you rarely know what other people are thinking or feeling. Their reactions are shaped by their own pressures, insecurities, workloads, and personal lives – not you. And yes, there may have been moments in the past when your assumptions turned out to be true. But one true assumption does not make every assumption true. Past experiences do not define every situation, every person, or every outcome.

**Notice how often you are creating assumptions.** You don't speak up in the meeting because you assume your idea isn't good enough; you don't apply for a job role because you assume you won't get it; you don't ask for feedback because you assume it will be bad. **Making assumptions may feel protective, but it quietly**

**shrinks your presence.** The brain treats imagined judgements as real, which is why it's important to consider this. Your nervous system reacts to a thought in the same way it would react to the situation actually happening. So when you assume rejection before it happens, your body responds with fear, avoidance and self-doubt. Your brain then begins to look for evidence to justify a belief that may not even be true.

For example, a certain look your colleague gave you may have had no subtext to it, but if you have a belief that people in the workplace don't like you, your brain will register that 'look' as false evidence to prove your belief is true. In reality, that 'look' could have been unintentional, with no malicious motive.

**Instead of assuming the worst, assume the best.**

Assumptions are simply thoughts, not facts; if you have no evidence – it is an assumption. Our minds will quickly think of the worst-case scenario, due to our brain's programming to protect us; however, if we can catch where we're just *assuming*, we can actively change that thought into a positive, reality-based assumption.

| *Scenario* | *Assumption* | *Reality-based assumption* | *Grounded action* |
|---|---|---|---|
| A colleague ignores your email. | *They've not replied to my email; they must think I'm being an inconvenience.* | *They may be busy with other tasks and haven't seen it yet. They will reply to me when they get the chance.* | Follow up politely when enough time has passed, without over-apologising or withdrawing. |
| You are left out of a work meeting. | *They've left me out because they don't value my contribution.* | *The meeting may not require my role, and not attending means I can prioritise my own workload.* | Ask for clarity about when your input is needed rather than assuming exclusion means you're not valued. |
| A colleague gives you a funny look. | *They don't like me.* | *They may be stressed or dealing with something right now.* | Continue working as normal; ask for feedback if necessary. |

**If a problem isn't communicated, then there is no problem.**

Doing mental backflips trying to guess what we *might* have done wrong or why the vibe is off drains our energy. If someone hasn't communicated a problem, then accept that there is no problem.

If someone doesn't have the courage or emotional maturity to communicate a problem, it is not your responsibility to go above and beyond trying to solve the issue (that's if there even is one; remember what I said earlier – we are not mind-readers!).

If you ask someone if everything's all right and they say 'yes', even if you think they're lying, take that answer at face value. **You cannot be responsible for other people's problems that they do not wish to communicate.**

Here are another few scenario examples, so you can practise those reality-based assumptions and take grounded actions!

| *Scenario* | *Assumption* | *Reality-based assumption* | *Grounded action* |
|---|---|---|---|
| Someone disagrees with your idea. | *My idea was bad.* | *They have a different perspective to me.* | Engage in discussion without self-attacking or shutting down. |
| You are rejected after trying for a promotion. | *I was rejected because I'm not good enough.* | *Promotion decisions are often based on timing, budget and role fit – and this rejection is not based on your inability to do the role.* | Ask for feedback if necessary, continue building relevant skills, and keep applying for roles that align with your growth. What is meant for you won't pass you by, and sometimes a rejection is simply making space for something that suits you better. |
| You're asked to revise work. | *I am incompetent at my role.* | *Revisions don't take away from the positive work you've already done; they just allow for collaboration and quality control.* | Continue to revise the work and ask for feedback if necessary. |

### *A Simple Assumption Checker*

Whenever you find yourself assuming something in the workplace that doesn't benefit you or make you feel empowered, ask yourself:

1. What am I assuming right now?
2. What evidence do I have?
3. What is the most neutral explanation?

My first vivid memory of overcoming my assumptions in the workplace is when I worked at a veterinary surgery. I was around nineteen years old, and I had left full-time education and landed a role doing an animal-care apprenticeship, which I loved. However, inside and outside this practice were lots of CCTV cameras.

In the boss's office, there was a big walled display of screens right in front of his desk, showcasing the CCTV. It was a well-known thing that the boss would monitor the CCTV screens to see where people were or what they were up to. Some of my colleagues would even go into his office just to see where people were.

Of course, having CCTV in any building is a normal safety protocol, but because I knew it was regularly being watched, I often felt self-conscious. If I was ever doing something that could be seen as something I shouldn't – for example, nipping to the staffroom or talking about topics unrelated to work with colleagues – I felt like there were eyes burning into the back of my head. At this point in my life, I hadn't done any kind of rejection therapy, so I was dealing with this underlying fear of being misperceived and misunderstood.

Sometimes, in the middle of the day, I'd nip back and forth to get things out of my car. I would never do it at an inappropriate time and I wouldn't do it often but, whenever I went to the car park, I felt like I was being watched – even if I wasn't. Now, here's the part that is relevant – I was assuming I was being watched and imagining what my manager was thinking – that he was wondering what I was doing. I was afraid I was going to get told off. I never had any factual evidence for this (yes, it was a fact that there were a load of CCTV screens in his office), and I'd never actually been 'told off' or pulled up for anything I was doing when I assumed I was being watched.

One day, I went to the car park to grab my water bottle. As usual, I felt this rush of anxiety, as if I was being watched and doing something I shouldn't. I was trying to be quick, so I wouldn't get in trouble, when I suddenly had a revelation.

**If I'm *assuming* I'm being watched right now, then I can *assume* I'm not being watched, because that's all this is: an assumption.**

The moment was like an epiphany: I had no evidence that my manager was watching me. Yes, he had those screens in his office, but who was I to know if he was monitoring them 24/7?

Even if he did watch me go to the car park, it didn't automatically mean he was thinking anything bad about it. The workplace wasn't a prison and he wasn't a nasty boss. I was just creating all these anxiety-inducing assumptions – and in doing so, something as simple as walking to and from my work car park had turned into a situation filled with apprehension.

As soon as I made that tiny little mindset-shift, the anxiety melted away. It felt profound. I couldn't believe how simple it was for me to change my entire internal state by simply not assuming the worst.

I started to notice where I was making assumptions in other situations at work too. There was a big gate to close and lock at the end of the working day, and sometimes it was my responsibility to lock it. It was right next to a busy road with cars flying past and I always felt so self-conscious that all the people in the cars were staring at me trying to lock this gate. Much like before, I was assuming the worst – that they were all staring at me – with no proof! So, the next time it was my turn to lock the gate, I reprogrammed my thinking and assumed no one in their cars was watching me. Guess what... I didn't feel self-conscious!

Similarly, as I was an apprentice, I was learning on the job. Because of this, I would often assume that I was doing things the wrong way. I'd also assume that people were getting annoyed at me, thinking I was a burden, or worse, talking badly about me behind my back. Then I started to assume the opposite. I chose to assume that people thought I was really good at my role, that they enjoyed teaching me, didn't think I was a burden, were kind and respectful about me, and weren't watching and critiquing my every move. And guess what… my anxiety melted away, slowly but surely. I started to feel more confident in my role, and felt positive and happy to be at work, all thanks to that simple mindset trick: changing my assumptions.

We don't realise how many unnecessary battles of anxiety we put ourselves through by automatically assuming the worst. Start to notice where *you* are making assumptions about things, situations or people in your life. Become aware of an assumption and actively change it to the opposite – something more empowering, and just watch how your confidence and happiness begins to improve for the better.

## WHAT DO YOU DO WHEN THERE IS EVIDENCE FOR YOUR SUSPICIONS?

On the other hand, sometimes there is evidence. Your boss arranges a meeting with you to discuss your performance; someone rudely interrupts you in a meeting; or your manager says something in front of the rest of the team that feels devaluing.

No matter how capable you are or how hard you try, these situations can be unavoidable. You can do everything 'right' and still encounter negative feedback, tension or poor behaviour from others. So, how do you handle these moments without letting them derail your confidence or drain your motivation?

The key is this: **do not attach your self-worth to them.** Feedback, other people's behaviour and workplace dynamics are information – not a reflection on your value.

**If you can't control it, don't let it control you.**

When these moments in the workplace happen, there are four things you can do (rather than fall into the rabbit hole of assumptions and anxiety) to make yourself feel at ease. These steps are not about excusing people's poor behaviour; they're about reframing the situation to avoid inner harm. From there, you can move forward and navigate the situation with more clarity and calmness.

1. **Separate evidence from interpretation**
   When something happens, our minds add meaning. For example, if your manager criticises your work publicly, your interpretation may be: 'They do not respect me.' Here, it's important to pause and ask yourself: 'What did I observe and what meaning am I adding?'

Name what happened without attaching meaning to it. That way, rather than internalising it as, 'They don't respect me,' you'll reframe this and describe it in a way that's neutral.

For example, let's say you're interrupted multiple times in a meeting. Neutral language keeps your nervous system regulated and prevents spiralling, stopping you from attaching *their* behaviour to *your* self-worth.

2 **Separate performance from identity**
Performance can be adjusted. Identity does not need attacking. For example, thinking something like, 'This presentation didn't go as intended,' is very different from thinking, 'I am bad at presenting. I'm never going to do that again. I'm so embarrassed – my team probably think I looked stupid.' One describes an outcome. The other attacks your sense of self. Choose the statement that describes the outcome. Remember, you are allowed to make mistakes; you are allowed to be bad at something; you are allowed to wish it went better than expected. What's not OK is attacking yourself every time you feel like you failed – you're human, not a robot.

3 **Ask outcome-focused questions when there is evidence**

Curiosity is more useful than self-blame. Instead of reverting to the latter, ask yourself helpful questions like, 'What is expected here? What would success look like in this context?' When there is a gap in information alignment or communication, ask questions that focus on improving next time without becoming self-critical.

4 **Keep your self-respect while adjusting**
Especially relevant in new jobs. You can adapt without attacking yourself. It's possible for you to say, 'No problem, I will make these revisions,' without falling into defensiveness, for example, 'That work I produced was terrible. I'm so bad at this role.' You don't need to over-apologise for being new at something. You don't need to over-apologise for making mistakes. Be kind to yourself and give yourself time to adjust. Remember, everyone's a beginner at some point.

## DEALING WITH DISAGREEMENTS IN THE WORKPLACE

Disagreements at work are inevitable. Not everyone will get on with you, understand you, or work well with you. Sometimes personalities, values or communication styles clash. This is common in the workplace because there's such an array of people, all with different backgrounds, experiences and insecurities. That can feel really hard to deal with, especially when the majority of us spend most of our time working.

When someone doesn't like us, it triggers our fight-or-flight response, and our survival instincts kick in. Being in a work environment makes our brains feel like we're part of a tribe – which I mentioned earlier. For survival purposes, our brains say we must be part of the tribe to survive, and the workplace mimics that, so when someone appears not to like us – whether by acting off, being passive aggressive or gossiping, it can very easily lead to feelings of stress, anxiety, and a dread of going into work.

Everyone responds to disagreements, confrontation and not being liked differently. Some people can easily shrug it off, but to many it's stressful and can affect how we show up in our job. Our minds panic and try to figure out the reason why someone may behave the way they do, and it can often turn into self-blame. In this case, it's important to remember: **incompatibility isn't a reflection of you.**

The healthiest way to deal with this kind of rejection is to stop trying to be chosen by everybody. In a professional environment, you're not going to experience universal approval. When someone does not like you, your task is not to win them over, but to remain respectful of your boundaries, remain consistent, clearly communicate on your shared goals and do your job well. You can acknowledge the tension without personalising it and, if anything, that person's behaviour says more about them than about your worth. **Learning to tolerate being disliked without self-abandonment is a powerful form of confidence, and it allows you to stay grounded, effective and present, even when harmony is not possible.** This takes practice. Disagreements naturally spike our anxiety and disrupt our nervous system. However, the goal here is not to take it as a personal attack – this isn't reflective of you or your character. Sometimes, it's just a matter of understanding and accepting that some personalities can – and do – clash.

You cannot control other people's behaviour, but you can control how you respond. When someone doesn't like us, it is easy to go into yearning mode. Where we start people-pleasing, being extra-nice, and overcompensate to regain their approval. But there is a difference between keeping the peace and abandoning yourself.

If somebody is rude to you at work, you do not have to go above and beyond to try and make that person like you. Let people show you who they are without internalising or seeing it as reflective of your worth. Keep the relationship professional, maintain your boundaries, and, remember: you go to work to make money and do your job well – not to be liked by everyone.

### *Gossiping in the Workplace*

Gossiping in the workplace seems to be normalised but it definitely shouldn't be. When it's repeated or targeted, it can cross into a subtle form of bullying. Most of us have been on the receiving end of gossip at some point in our lives, so we all know how isolating, upsetting and confidence-knocking it can feel.

What many people don't realise is that gossip often comes from insecurity. In certain workplace dynamics, if someone feels threatened by another person, that insecurity can turn into jealousy. Some people lack the self-awareness to recognise what they're feeling, and instead of addressing it, they try to relieve their discomfort by dragging someone else down.

As someone who has experienced this dynamic first-hand, I know how painful it can feel when you sense people turning against you, especially when you believe you've done nothing wrong. And sometimes you *haven't* done anything wrong. At other times you may have – and that's OK, you're allowed to apologise.

*Staying Professional*

Professionalism means staying regulated when outcomes are uncertain. What's important is maintaining your confidence, and knowing that even if you, your ideas or beliefs are not chosen, that doesn't symbolise anything about *you*.

Handling rejection well at work is a skill and, like any skill, it improves with practice. Responding professionally does not mean pretending you are unaffected; it means choosing behaviour that serves your long-term goals. This might look like thanking someone for their time, asking for feedback if appropriate, or continuing to contribute with consistency rather than withdrawing. It can look like talking to someone after work – whether your partner, a friend or a trusted person – and sharing how that rejection made you feel. You are allowed to experience emotion when you're rejected. What's important is to practise not taking it personally, and not applying a meaning to said rejection that you have no evidence for. Every single time you choose a better narrative, you are building your self-confidence.

When it comes to navigating 'no's, it's easy to shrink yourself. Many people choose to disappear after they hear the word 'no' – sharing less and mentally stepping back. But here's the thing: what you *should* do is actually the opposite. One of the most powerful things you can do after experiencing rejection is remaining visible. Staying visible after rejection communicates resilience – it shows that your engagement is not conditional on validation. This particularly applies in work meetings and group discussions.

Building confidence at work is built through repetition, not perfection. Each time you respond calmly instead of collapsing inwards and attacking yourself, you reinforce trust in yourself. Over time, you'll learn that your worth is not defined by acceptance or rejection.

## REJECTION THERAPY AT WORK

Rejection therapy can be especially useful in a professional environment, when done thoughtfully and efficiently. The goal is not to provoke rejection recklessly, but to reduce fear around asking, contributing and being seen at work.

Rejection therapy might look like asking questions you would normally hold back from putting forward, pitching ideas even if they may not land, requesting feedback, or applying for roles that feel slightly out of reach. Each ask is exposure, and every time you do this, it teaches your nervous system that rejection is survivable.

When I began practising this intentionally, something shifted. I stopped waiting to feel confident about acting. I acted while feeling unsure and learned that discomfort did not equal danger. Most of the time I was pleasantly surprised. I contributed an idea in a group setting – one that I'd usually avoid speaking up in – and it was received positively. So much so that my manager took the idea and made it into a successful social-media campaign.

I kept speaking up, and my suggestions to improve work dynamics or to establish clearer working boundaries for myself were positively accepted and valued. It came as a surprise. I started to realise how much I was holding myself back and limiting my potential, out of fear of being judged.

Now that I was receiving a positive response, I wasn't internalising fear as much – and it made me realise just that – it was fear holding me back. When you stop assuming and start stepping into the belief that there is no harm in asking, you'll start to become pleasantly surprised. Over time, the emotional charge around rejection will soften and the word 'no' loses its power.

# 12

## Rejection in Relationships

Rejection in relationships can feel like the most personal kind. When someone doesn't choose you, pulls away or can't meet you where you're at, it can feel like a direct reflection of your worth, making you feel like you're simply not good enough.

Romantic and platonic rejection tends to hit deeper because it touches our primal instinct to be desired; the feeling of wanting to belong, be chosen, be seen, accepted as we are, and loved unconditionally.

When rejection happens in relationships, many of us don't just grieve the loss of the connection – we grieve our imagined future. The 'ideal' future we create in our minds, our plan of what we thought would happen, is suddenly turned on its head. We grieve the version of ourselves that the relationship gave us. When it comes to being rejected by a person we cared about, we grieve the feeling of being chosen by that person.

In moments like this, your mind can instantly jump to thinking, 'What is wrong with me?' It's easy to spiral into negative self-talk: 'Maybe if I looked a certain way, behaved differently, sent that text or didn't say that thing, maybe they would have chosen me.'

The mind creates endless stories of why we possibly weren't chosen, beating ourselves up, but here's the truth: **not being chosen isn't a reflection of your worth.**

The aim here isn't to analyse yourself into exhaustion; it's to interrupt the stories. To stop personalising outcomes that were never meant to define you, and to loosen the belief that rejection means something is wrong with you.

Not being chosen doesn't mean you're ugly, weird, boring, not good enough, intimidating or whatever your mind tells you are. When you aren't chosen, remind yourself that the story you're telling yourself is not a fact.

Learning to experience relationship rejections without turning it into self-rejection is a skill. It's about staying connected to your worth, even when your heart hurts and your ego is bruised. It's about understanding that rejection, as painful as it can be, may later become one of the most meaningful turning points in your life.

## WHY DOES RELATIONSHIP REJECTION STING SO MUCH?

Romantic and platonic relationships often become mirrors. We look to them for validation, reassurance and confirmation that we are enough. When a relationship ends or doesn't develop, the mind searches for meaning, often at the expense of our worth. Rather than looking at the reason for the relationship's failure, or inability to progress, as a result of a mismatch in needs, timing, compatibility or capacity – or the other person's lack of availability or unwillingness – it's easy for your brain to feed you a story about your value instead.

Here's what you need to do when you notice this cropping up: **fall in love with rejection.**

Ask yourself, 'Why would I want to be chosen by somebody who doesn't choose me?' Rather than internalising rejection as a reflection of your worth, transform your thinking. Show gratitude for the rejection, because why would you *want* to be with someone who doesn't choose *you* fully? Yes, naturally we want to be chosen, but this is the whole point of this book: **not being chosen isn't a reflection on your worth.**

Your goal is to build such high self-respect and trust within yourself that if you are not chosen, you don't see this as something being 'wrong' with you; it simply means you and that person aren't compatible (and that's OK!). Incompatibility can feel disappointing – I'm not saying this to dismiss that. But often the disappointment you feel isn't about the person themselves, but the potential you saw in them, and the imagined futures and stories you attached to them.

In other words, we often grieve the idea of someone, not the reality shown to us.

Sometimes we can be completely blindsided by someone's rejection. Everything might have, seemingly, been going great. Maybe the person was saying all the right things, getting you excited for the future, only to then rip the rug from beneath you and call it off. Of course, that's going to hurt.

Being able to handle rejection doesn't mean we aren't allowed to feel our feelings (we totally are!). We get attached to people and when that ends, it's normal to feel upset about it. It's important not to dismiss how you feel – you're a human and your feelings need to be felt – however, we can feel our feelings without turning them into a self-deprecating blame game.

Let people show us who they are. If someone doesn't choose you, that's not a bad thing. In fact, it's because of this that you will likely meet someone who does choose you. You can't meet the right person by being with the wrong one. You want somebody to choose you because they love your authenticity, the way you carry yourself, the values you hold, the ambitions you have, the hobbies you love. If someone doesn't choose you, that is not a loss. It is simply making space for the person who will.

It's also worth remembering that just because one person doesn't choose you, it doesn't mean nobody else will. We often fall into a lack mindset, where we think things like 'all the good ones are taken', but let me reassure you – there are more than enough people to go around for everyone.

The universe is abundant, there are eight **billion** people on this planet (a number our minds can't truly comprehend) and of these, there are thousands of people who would happily choose you, appreciate you and be drawn to exactly who you are. And when you meet your person (key word: when – because you will), you will be so thankful it didn't work out with anyone else. Don't let one person's inability to choose you define how you see the rest of the world.

**There is plenty of love to go around.**

Instead of taking rejection personally, see it as a process of elimination. When someone doesn't want to go on a second date or they don't give you their number, that doesn't need to be internalised as a self-attack. Simply thank them for not wasting your time and be proud of yourself for having the courage to get out of your comfort zone in the first place.

We are way too quick to fall into self-criticism and self-abandonment when we get rejected, but focus on the silver linings. Empower yourself! Look at the positives from that situation. Asking someone for their number, regardless of the outcome, will build your courage, confidence and resilience. You've proved to your brain, 'I can do scary things and survive' – that should be celebrated!

**Regardless of the outcome, there is always a silver lining. Find it.**

Rejection isn't part of your identity. Getting rejected shouldn't make you feel embarrassed; it should make you feel empowered for having the courage to ask. You miss 100 per cent of the shots you don't take and you're more likely to find your person by asking than letting the opportunity pass you by.

**Rejection doesn't need to be overcomplicated – it is just communication.**

'No' isn't inherently negative; it is simply another person communicating. It's no different from hearing 'yes'. Words are just a collection of different sounds and symbols all strung together, so humans can communicate. We put meanings onto them. To take your power back when you hear a 'no' in a relationship dynamic, try putting your own meaning on it. Let it mean something empowering, rather than belittling.

**'No' is just a two-letter word – nothing else.**

Respect the 'no', take a deep breath and carry on with your day. A word can't hurt you unless you give it permission to do so.

## REJECTION ≠ YOU'RE NOT LOVEABLE

Rejection is not the same as being unloveable. One of the most important shifts you can make is learning to separate rejection from your identity. Someone can like you and still not choose you; someone can care about you and still not be able to show up consistently; someone can think you're a great person and not want to be in a relationship with you.

Here are some examples.

| *Scenario* | *Example* | *What this means* |
|---|---|---|
| *Right person, wrong time* | Someone can care deeply about you, but may have other things going on – focusing on their career, grieving a loved one, focusing on their mental health and personal growth, etc. | Rejection is based on their current circumstances, not your value or desirability. You never know what people are going through; someone can genuinely like you and not be able to show up in the way a relationship requires. |
| *Different attachment styles* | You may want closeness and consistency while the other person needs distance. | Rejection is based on different attachment styles; neither style is wrong, but the incompatibility can make connection painful or unsustainable. |
| *Incompatible life goals* | One wants children and commitment while the other person wants to travel the world. | Rejection is based on different life goals, values and priorities; neither is right or wrong, but the goals do not align to allow the relationship to flourish. |
| *Emotional availability* | Someone can be attracted to you and like you, but they may be healing from a past relationship, unresolved trauma or consistent unhealthy patterns in relationships. | Rejection is not because they don't like you but because they feel unable to participate in a healthy relationship right now. |

| *Scenario* | *Example* | *What this means* |
|---|---|---|
| *Chemistry without compatibility* | Maybe you are wildly attracted to one another but your communication, emotional safety and values don't align. | Rejection is because you need more than physical attraction to sustain a healthy relationship. Compatibility matters more than intensity. |
| *Authentic self-expression* | You communicated your needs, boundaries or feelings and it wasn't received in the way you hoped. | Rejection that follows authenticity is information, not a negative reflection of your worth. It reveals compatibility, capacity or maturity. It doesn't mean something is 'wrong' with you. The right person will have no problem with your authentic expression – in fact, they'll encourage it. |

Rejection often says more about fit and timing than it ever does about your worth. It's not a case of, 'Well, if they liked me enough, they would choose me.' This belief is damaging because liking someone is not the same as being available to them in a romantic sense. Choice is influenced by a number of things, as we've touched on, from personal preferences to emotional capacity.

When it comes to romantic relationships, attraction and a willingness to pursue the relationship needs to be mutual. If you find yourself rejected by someone, don't fall into the trap of expecting them to change their mind. Respect and accept their rejection, sit with your feelings, and then, when you're ready, pick yourself back up and carry on with your life. Invest in things that make you happy, prioritise friendships, explore new hobbies or passions, and seek out opportunities for adventure; the world is your oyster when you're single. **You have your own life to fall in love with.** The right person will find you when the time is right.

**You don't need someone to 'complete you': you already are complete.**

Holding onto hope and waiting for someone can quietly turn into a self-fulfilling prophecy. You may wait for them to be 'ready', only to discover that your values still don't align. In the meantime, the longer you wait, the more emotional energy you invest, which can deepen feelings of abandonment or rejection when things don't change.

Let people show you who they are and take that information at face value, without turning it into a personal flaw. **Waiting doesn't create alignment.** And by waiting for the wrong person, you may be delaying the opportunity to meet the right person.

## STOP CHASING

Many of us often subconsciously learn to measure our worth by how wanted we are. Attention becomes reassurance, and being chosen becomes proof that you're 'good enough'. When your self-esteem depends on external validation, rejection can feel unbearable. And this is through no fault of our own. It's what society has conditioned us to believe.

What we need instead is a self-esteem rooted in how we see ourselves, not in who chooses us. A sense of worth that stays steady whether we're in a relationship or not. When your value comes from within, rejection may still hurt, but it no longer defines you.

When you stop chasing validation in romantic relationships and choose to validate yourself, you radiate a different kind of light and confidence. Everything you desire to feel from another person, you can feel yourself. When you no longer rely on other people to make you feel loved and decide to love yourself, you'll stop tolerating the bare minimum.

**You don't need 'another half' to be 'whole'.**

You are born whole: you are not born with a part of you missing that has to be found within another person. Think of how loved babies are – how much people coddle and coo over them. In their natural state, they are pure, innocent, magical beings. We don't look at them and think, 'If only they had someone else to make them whole.' Imagine if you could look at yourself with the same awe and love. You deserve that love too.

As we go through life getting emotionally battered and bruised, it's easy for us to compare ourselves, to feel empty and to believe that the only way we can fill that emptiness is by being with another person. But the truth is, being in a relationship or being single doesn't define you. You are still whole, you are still magic and you are still loveable.

If you find yourself in this frame of mind, it might be time to turn inwards. Here are five self-love journal prompts to help you move towards internal validation. These will help to strengthen your inner voice, and encourage you to think and feel more empowered.

1 What makes me feel most alive and joyful?
2 How have I grown in the past year?
3 What is one thing I can do today, this week, and this month, that my future self will thank me for?
4 What three things do I love about myself?
5 How would my best friend describe me?

Loving yourself is a journey that can feel uncomfortable at times, but it's something anyone can start practising at any time. We all need to give ourselves more self-love.

When you learn to validate yourself, to appreciate your beauty, to value your personality, relationships become a bonus in your life. When you realise that you're already whole and see a partner as an addition to your life – someone who makes it richer, inspires and supports you – it takes you out of a space of seeking someone out of desperation. You are not broken; you are not lacking anything. When you're validated from within, you can approach relationships in a grounded and abundant way, which will allow you to find a partner who aligns with you.

## AUTHENTICITY IS YOUR MAGNET

It's a painful reality, but many of us hide parts of ourselves to avoid rejection. We soften our opinions, downplay our needs, shrink our intensity and carefully curate our dating profiles, upload our best pictures to look appealing, and share relatable prompts in a bid to attract people. We believe that if we become agreeable and palatable, we will get chosen – but this strategy comes at a cost.

When you reject yourself to avoid being rejected by others, you lose your connection to your most powerful gift – your authenticity. And while we may believe that we have to show up as an edited or curated version of ourselves in the early stages of dating, to 'perform our best' in order to be chosen, this is far from the truth.

You want to be so unapologetically yourself that your authenticity becomes your magnet for finding the right people. This isn't just for romantic relationships; it applies to platonic relationships too. Being authentic, whether that's owning your interests, showcasing your fashion style, not hiding your personality quirks, and being clear about your needs and desires, will repel *some* people, but it will also attract the *right* people.

**Be yourself, so the right people can find you**

Authenticity is not about oversharing or demanding acceptance; it's being so aligned with who you are that you feel able to communicate and express yourself in a way that feels right. It's about reconnecting with yourself beyond social conditioning and expectations, trauma, relationship breakdowns, and needs you've silenced.

You weren't put on this earth to be a carbon copy of everyone else. You were divinely crafted to be exactly who YOU are, so honour that. Allow your true personality to be seen, and if someone doesn't choose that, oh well! They are simply not your person. Those who you're more aligned with will find you.

**Let your light shine so brightly that the right people can find you.**

True connection can't form when you're showing up as a version of you that is edited. If someone is only attracted to you when you pretend to be something you're not, the relationship will require ongoing self-abandonment to survive. **Start the relationship as you mean to go on by being unapologetically yourself.**

In the next chapter, we'll be looking at what happens when rejection doesn't go to plan but, before we do, here are some tips to practise rejection therapy in your relationships – whether platonic or romantic:

1. **Express your interest instead of waiting.** Say you enjoyed someone's company; ask for their number or another way to continue the connection; compliment someone without thinking about the outcome. The win is expressing your truth, not reciprocation.
2. **Ask for clarity early to avoid feeling confused later down the line.** Ask where you stand, if you're unclear. Name your needs without apologising. For example, 'I value consistency and regular communication.' Remember, your needs are not a burden and you are allowed to express them unapologetically.
3. **Set a boundary.** Say no to anything that doesn't feel right.
4. **Initiate plans.** Invite someone to do something. You don't need to add a soft pillow, in case they reject you (e.g. saying, 'No worries if not!'). Rather than anticipating rejection, simply invite them to do something and allow

them to answer in a way that feels authentic to them.

5 Be OK with a 'no'. If someone says 'no', whether in a romantic or platonic environment, respond with dignity. Thank them for being honest and leave the situation with your head held high. This will help you grow self-trust, confidence and self-respect.

# 13

## When It Doesn't Go to Plan

Rejection therapy is empowering, freeing and even exhilarating at times, but there are moments when it doesn't go as planned. In these moments, rejection can feel sharper than expected. When the response is awkward, dismissive or emotionally loaded, your body reacts before your mind can catch up and instead of feeling brave, you feel exposed, embarrassed and possibly shaky.

While rejection therapy will help you deal with rejection, build your confidence and make you more resilient, it can also bring you face to face with the very fear you were trying to avoid – provoking feelings you're not used to. When that happens, the goal is not to 'toughen up' or simply push through; it's about learning how to respond in a way that protects your self-worth, helps your nervous system settle, and turns a painful moment into something meaningful.

One of the most confronting and anxiety-inducing parts of rejection therapy is the fact you cannot control or fully predict how a rejection will land. You may prepare logically and tell yourself, 'It's just a challenge.' You can reassure yourself that you're not going to die; it's not personal, yet your body still might react with a flushed face, shaky hands or a tight chest. You might experience wanting the ground to swallow you up, feel uncomfortable and awkward, or have the urge to disappear from the situation immediately.

When this happens, it doesn't mean that rejection therapy has failed. It doesn't mean you're weak and not capable of doing it. It just means you are human. It's important that we are kind to ourselves, allow our reactions to situations to happen without judgement, honour our nervous systems and show ourselves some compassion.

**Discomfort does not last for ever.**

We avoid discomfort at all costs. We fill the awkward silences, avoid having honest conversations with our partners, friends and loved ones, and dismiss our own needs to 'keep the peace'. We stay seated instead of getting up on the dance floor to avoid feeling silly; we change our outfits if they seem 'too much', and tone down our personalities so we do not 'stand out'.

Humans hate discomfort. Our brains interpret unfamiliar or awkward moments as potential threats, even when there is no real danger. We never give ourselves a chance to build our tolerance to it. So, our ability to deal with it remains low because as soon as we feel it, we run away in the opposite direction. But what if you gave yourself more opportunities to be uncomfortable and learn, so that you can handle it?

When we avoid discomfort, we don't have a sense of how it feels for it to pass naturally. We don't experience the relief that comes from realising, 'This is uncomfortable, but I'm OK'. The discomfort continues to feel overwhelming, even in situations that are ultimately harmless. But here's the thing – yes, **being uncomfortable isn't the most enjoyable feeling in the world, but it does always pass.**

This is where rejection therapy comes in. It offers a safe, intentional way to build your tolerance for discomfort. By intentionally stepping into small moments of awkwardness or potential rejection, you teach your nervous system that discomfort is not danger. You learn that you can feel exposed, embarrassed or uncertain, and still be safe.

Rejection therapy isn't about forcing yourself into distress. It's about **gently expanding your capacity to sit with discomfort, so it no longer controls your choices.** And over time, what once felt unbearable becomes manageable. What once felt terrifying starts to feel freeing, and that's how you begin to stop holding yourself back. Practising rejection therapy gives you a key you can use to unlock doors that previously would have remained closed – out of the fear of embarrassment, discomfort or fear.

So, don't rush to fill the awkward silence: communicate your needs clearly, even if your voice shakes; sing karaoke; dance badly; crack a dad joke to the cashier and let your discomfort pass naturally. Discomfort isn't something to eliminate; it's something to move through. You may not be in control of when discomfort shows up, but you are always in control of how you respond to it. Every time you stay present instead of escaping it, you're telling your nervous system, 'I can handle it.'

**An awkward silence is only awkward if you say it's awkward.**

## WHEN DISCOMFORT LINGERS LONGER THAN EXPECTED

Maybe you've removed yourself from the situation, a few hours have passed – and you still feel a heavy discomfort. Use that information to learn more about yourself. Ask yourself, 'Why did that affect me so much?'

There were two rejection therapy challenges that I did that left me with more discomfort than others. In those instances, I came home after the interactions and still felt embarrassed, anxious. Both were great opportunities to learn more about myself and expose hidden wounds or insecurities that I didn't even know I had.

The first one was on day three of rejection therapy. It really was a pivotal point. It was the start of my thirty-day rejection therapy journey, and I went into a well-known takeaway and asked if I could help deliver pizzas. The lady thought I was asking for a job, and I didn't have the confidence to stand in the discomfort and tell the truth, so instead I said, 'Yeah, I'm just looking for a job.' I wrote down my number, gave it to her and went home.

Hours after the interaction happened, I was lying on my bed still feeling this gut-wrenching embarrassment, replaying the moment in my head. I asked myself, 'Why is this bothering me so much?' and ultimately found that it boiled down to the fear of being perceived in a way that didn't align with my true personality; essentially, a fear of being misunderstood. It was the fact I walked out of that pizza shop and the lady who served me had the opportunity to potentially think something wrong about me. That was what was causing me my continued discomfort and anxiety.

The idea of this woman having the wrong perception was a stumbling block – it felt like an attack on my identity, which I'd been building for years and protecting. It challenged the way I wanted other people to see me and I didn't like that. I felt an overwhelming urge to justify why I'd gone into the pizza shop and asked such an odd question. I wanted to prove to this stranger who I *really* was, to correct her misperception of me. It was a profound realisation to have, because I realised that I had a fear of being misunderstood. Suddenly the dots started to connect and I realised for a lot of my life, I'd been showing up in the world as an edited version of myself. I created this identity that I liked, and that was the only way I wanted other people to see me. If anything jeopardised that, it would send me into deep stress and panic.

I realised this was a protection mechanism I'd built due to going through certain traumas as a teenager. I had been so deeply misunderstood back then that I never wanted to be misunderstood again. If I was, my fight-or-flight panic response would kick in. I had learned that if someone misjudged me, it subconsciously threatened my survival.

It suddenly became so evident that I carried this fear throughout school, college, my previous jobs, relationships, even my friendships. This fear of only being able to show up in a way where people liked me consumed my everyday life, and I had no idea.

When I came to this realisation, I literally felt the discomfort wash away. It was as if that part of me had been screaming to be looked at, to be shown some love and care. When it had finally been identified, I could soothe myself.

I coached my way through this fear, asking myself, 'Even though I may have been misunderstood, was

I still safe?' Of course, the answer was yes. From that moment, in every rejection therapy challenge, my fight-or-flight reaction slowly eased. Any potential confusion didn't feel emotionally charged because after every challenge, I was still coming home alive and breathing. My brain was learning that being misunderstood was not dangerous.

I learned that what other people thought of me only had power if I gave it permission to. Quite quickly, I started to witness myself unmask in my everyday life – dancing to the music in the supermarket, reaching out to old friends I hadn't seen in years, letting my personality shine more, going to a gym class and standing at the front. I was no longer showing up in the world 'edited'. I allowed myself to show authentically in a way that felt aligned and true to me.

Of course, having this initial reaction of discomfort when doing a challenge wasn't ideal – it definitely didn't feel pleasant! – but that moment changed my life for the better. By sitting with discomfort and not running away from it, I learned something really important about myself.

A helpful way to tell whether a challenge has triggered something beyond expected discomfort is to notice how long the embarrassment lasts afterwards. During rejection therapy, especially at the beginning, it's completely normal to feel a bit silly, awkward, exposed or uncomfortable in the moment. With grounding techniques, those feelings should settle fairly quickly. However, if a challenge leaves you feeling unusually distressed, stuck or emotionally shaken long after it's over, that's valuable information. It doesn't mean you've failed; it means something deeper may have been touched. You can use those moments as opportunities for self-awareness, reflection and growth, rather than pushing yourself further without listening.

The second challenge that stood out was when I was in a city-centre coffee shop. I thought, 'I need to do a rejection-therapy challenge today. What can I do? What's going to get me out of my comfort zone?'

There was a big open space outside the coffee shop with lots of people around, so I thought, 'Why don't I pretend to be a dog?' I didn't give it much thought; it just seemed well outside my comfort zone; I knew it would cause people to stare, and it seemed a bit out of the ordinary. In other words, it was perfect! So off I went into the middle of the city centre, heading outside on my hands and knees, in dog mode. I even made a few woof sounds.

It was the first challenge I did that instantly provoked negative reactions from passers-by. I had a scarf round my neck and because I had 'rejection therapy' in my mind, I asked a man to walk me, because I knew he'd likely say no. He looked disgusted at my request and walked off. I carried on crawling around and two teenage girls came over to me, started laughing and took a photo of me. They didn't say hi – they were laughing at me, and not in a nice way. Feeling embarrassed, I stood up and stopped doing the challenge. I didn't think much of the embarrassment at the time, as I assumed it would pass fairly quickly. (Just to note, this challenge took place a few months after I'd done my initial thirty-day challenge, so at this point I was fairly experienced with rejection therapy and knowing how to handle my emotions after a challenge.) When I got home quite a few hours later, I watched the video back to edit it and post on TikTok, still feeling embarrassed. But this was a new kind of embarrassment – one that I'd never experienced before. I sat with the feeling and tried to get to the bottom of why this challenge in particular had provoked such a strong reaction.

I realised that what I'd done didn't make me feel good about myself. By crawling on the floor and acting like a dog, I felt demoralised, and I hadn't realised this until I was doing it. Now, writing this down and reading it aloud, it seems obvious. Of course, crawling on the floor in a busy public space, woofing and asking strangers to walk me is demoralising, but at the time, in my head, I was thinking, 'People are definitely gonna say no to walking me.' My focus was on the rejection in the moment. I was a girl on a mission, and it wasn't until doing it that I realised it might actually be going too far. I hadn't considered the fact I could do rejection therapy without demeaning myself.

I can look back and laugh about it now. The world didn't stop spinning. The discomfort did indeed pass, and it was a good learning curve. The worst thing that could have happened did happen and I survived. Some girls laughed and took a photo of me; a man gave me a disgusted look, but I was, ultimately, fine. I went home afterwards; I was still breathing, and that situation didn't define me as a person. Overall, the challenge helped build my resilience. What I reflect on now, looking back, is that it was definitely something I shouldn't have done – and I wouldn't recommend doing anything that you feel is demoralising.

Receiving an odd look, abrupt response or an awkward silence is a part of rejection therapy. It sounds counterintuitive to say this, but when these things happen, they can actually be really helpful. The anticipation of an uncomfortable response from somebody else is often worse than it happening.

When the worst outcome does happen – let's say someone's staring at you or there's an awkward moment – you're building your resilience to be able to handle any situation. If you are faced with what you thought would be the worst response possible, and you survive it, your brain learns, 'I can handle it.'

People giving you funny looks during your rejection therapy journey is not something to be scared of. A look can't hurt you and doesn't mean there's anything negative about you or your character – a look is simply a look.

**People's reactions do not define you.**

Discovering you can move on from a negative response gives you a transferable skill that can be applied to every part of your everyday life. Just think how often you avoid sending an email because you want to avoid the potential discomfort. How often do you avoid asking for a pay rise? Or avoid changing plans to suit others? By trying to avoid an uncomfortable reaction, we often find it easier to say nothing at all, usually to the detriment of ourselves.

But when you've purposely exposed yourself to discomfort head-on, in a slow and controlled way, and you've taught yourself, 'I can handle it,' whatever the outcome, you know you'll be OK. You send the email anyway, ask for a pay rise with confidence, and cancel plans you're not up for because you trust yourself to be OK with whatever the reaction is – that is a life-changing skill.

## HOW TO REGULATE YOURSELF AFTER A CHALLENGE

Your first priority after a painful rejection is **regulation,** *not* reflection. If your nervous system is activated, your mind will not be able to reason clearly. Trying to make sense of the rejection while feeling dysregulated often leads to spiralling thoughts and harsh self-judgement.

Instead, focus on calming your body first. Slow your breathing, take deep breaths and ground yourself. Remind yourself that the moment has passed and you are safe. Something I tell myself often is, 'Nobody is thinking about it other than me,' which really helps.

I have a vivid memory of one example of regulating myself after a rejection therapy challenge (ironically, the challenge was one of my most viral videos!). I was on my first ever solo holiday to Portugal, flying for the first time on my own, and I was sitting near the front of the plane. I got this idea to stand up and tell everyone, 'Have a nice flight, everybody,' before the plane took off.

I'd never done a challenge like this before: standing up, making an announcement, drawing attention to myself with nowhere to escape. I had no one with me as a safety blanket and was sitting next to two complete strangers. I was super-nervous and I almost didn't do it. After five minutes of contemplation, I had a thought: 'If this scares you so much, that's a sign to do it.' I counted down from three, then stood up and announced, 'Have a lovely flight everybody. Here's to making memories.' I even finished my announcement with a little 'woo'.

Giggling to myself, I sat back down. My heart was pounding and I was physically shaking. I couldn't believe I'd done it. Obviously I couldn't leave the plane, so I had to sit in discomfort and regulate myself. The reaction from the other passengers wasn't negative; in fact, a few people giggled, but that didn't stop my body's natural response to produce adrenaline. For around five minutes afterwards, I felt very anxious. I could still feel my heart beating fast, and my hands were shaking, but as soon as I sat back down from making my announcement, I took deep breaths.

After five minutes, my body no longer felt dysregulated. My mind, however, was creating stories – about how silly I should feel – but I forced myself to think differently. I looked around to see if anyone was staring at me, and nobody was. Instead, everyone was carrying on as normal – in their own world, talking to their partners, doing word searches, reading books. Nobody was thinking about what I'd done other than me. It was the reassurance I needed. It was pointless to sit there for two hours feeling embarrassed. The only person it was affecting was me – nobody else cared.

**Embarrassment is a choice.**

If you've just completed a rejection therapy challenge and find yourself in a space you can't easily leave, a good way of regulating yourself is by taking deep breaths and reminding yourself that once the moment has passed, nobody else, other than you, will be thinking about it. It's a very simple mindset switch, but one that can melt away all your anxiety.

When you feel that sense of calm, that's the time to reflect and process the experience clearly. Ask yourself what you've learned and how it went. Avoid doing this when you feel dysregulated, because your brain will make it seem worse than it actually is.

What you are doing is not dangerous: you're not being rude – you have simply done something out of your comfort zone. However, your brain doesn't know the difference between jumping off a building or standing up on the train and telling everybody a joke. Fear is fear. The amygdala is activated, no matter the situation – whether you're in physical danger or not.

This is why it is so important to take baby steps and slowly build your exposure to rejection. You have to teach your brain to handle discomfort. The more challenges you do, the quieter the emotional charge becomes, and the quicker you are able to regulate yourself.

It got to a point after my thirty-day challenge where I could confidently ask anybody a question, expecting a 'no', and not feel any emotional charge. My brain became desensitised to hearing a 'no' or getting a funny look so that, to me, they were simply neutral experiences. I was no longer attaching a meaning to it.

It didn't affect my amygdala because my brain had learned that rejection is not dangerous. Yes, there may be times where it doesn't feel nice initially, but you're not physically threatened. We're just taught that it means something more than it should, so when we confront our fear of rejection head-on consistently – and in a controlled way – it loses its emotional charge and power. That is why it's so important to stick at the thirty-day rejection challenge, even when it feels hard – and especially at the beginning.

Remember to ask yourself, 'What actually happened and what story I am telling myself about it?

Often the event itself is simple – someone said 'no', someone politely declined, someone didn't respond as hoped – and the suffering comes from the meaning we attribute to it.

**The outcome does not define you.**

Rejection is a tool, not a weapon. Use rejection therapy as a tool for learning and tolerating uncertainty, not a weapon that you use not to speak up again or take risks. Rejection allows you to see where more self-love and compassion is needed, and can show you hidden areas of yourself that you could develop.

## KNOWING WHEN YOU NEED TO PAUSE

It's important to know when to step back. **Rejection therapy should stretch you, not overwhelm you.** If you find yourself consistently feeling dysregulated, ruminating or losing confidence, it may be time to slow down and pause. It's OK to repeat easier challenges or increase your recovery time. It's OK to need support from your friends or family. Rejection therapy can spike your nervous system, so it's important to handle that with care.

Listen to your needs and, even more importantly, listen to your body. If it's starting to feel too much, that doesn't mean you've failed or you're too weak. Everybody's tolerances and previous experiences are different, and when you step out of your comfort zone, everyone responds differently. Whichever way you respond is OK. Only you know what is too far. There's a fine line between feeling the typical nerves or anxious anticipation when you're about to do a challenge, and the feeling of doing 'too much' or going 'too far'. Only you will know the difference. Listen to that inner voice.

As I continued doing rejection therapy beyond my initial thirty-day challenge, there were times where I didn't want to do something. In those moments, the anxiety beforehand has been loud. In some of these instances, I've pushed through and it's not been as bad as I thought. In fact, in some moments, I felt really liberated afterwards. On the other hand, there are also times when I've been having a down day, or felt like life is on top of me, and I've known and trusted that voice that's told me I don't have the emotional capacity to do rejection therapy that day. That's OK! Only you know your limits, and it's OK to acknowledge them.

# 14

## How to Turn Rejection into Confidence

At this current moment, writing this chapter, I embarked on rejection therapy almost two years ago. After repeated, consistent, comfort-zone stretching, it's safe to say rejection therapy has changed my life. I never expected that a thirty-day challenge would transform me in the way it has. If someone told me in those first two weeks, when I was finding it really hard to do the challenges, that two years later I'd still be doing rejection therapy and be enjoying it, I simply would not have believed them.

The reason I'm still doing rejection therapy isn't because it hasn't worked – it's because it has. **My comfort zone has consistently expanded to a point where I'm doing things that younger me simply could not imagine.** The Sophie from two years ago would not believe that I went into a coffee shop with my handmade sock puppet, Mr Sickle, and ordered my coffee using him. She would not believe that I could sit on a train and start emotionally singing out of the window, pretending I'm in a real-life music video. She would not believe that I went to a supermarket in a wedding dress or approached a man I thought was good-looking and asked him on a date. She would not believe the hundreds of challenges I have done, because that level of confidence was something she could only dream of at the time.

That feeling becomes addictive. Nothing quite makes you feel alive like doing rejection therapy. For me, it's no longer a chore; it's a form of self-expression. It reminds me not to take life so seriously and shows me that life can be a playground. I really believe the world would be a lot happier if we all had more sprinkles of harmless fun in our day. It's a self-help challenge that reminds me I'm stronger than the invisible limitations my mind imposes. **I am stronger than the fear in my body.** I have realised I am so much braver than I ever thought I was.

But let me create no illusions. I haven't become completely immune to fear, but I have changed my relationship with it. Sometimes that little voice of doubt creeps in, but I have learned the skills not to let it hold me back, and now that skill naturally flows into my everyday life.

It was an accident that rejection therapy became my niche online. It was never strategic. I didn't even realise it would resonate with so many people. I was simply documenting my own journey of overcoming my fear of rejection and building my confidence.

When the thirty days came to an end, I didn't want to stop. I felt like there was more I could achieve, more ways I could grow, and I felt this liberation by not only proving to myself that I could do it, but also by inspiring other people to do it too.

When we see people going outside their comfort zone, it inspires us. We feel we can do the same. By watching me be bold with my rejection therapy challenges, my followers have seen that they, too, can do little things in life to stop holding themselves back. Watching me dress up in a cow costume to go to the gym has inspired some of my followers to simply go to the gym (in normal gym clothes, mind you) without fearing being judged. Watching me order my coffee using a sock puppet has helped some followers feel more confident when it comes to ordering their coffee on a typical day. Seeing me face public embarrassment on a regular basis – and survive it – has given people permission to stop living their life in fear of being judged.

Maybe some of you who are reading this book have never felt an ounce of social anxiety in your life and can't relate to this at all. To that, I say, lucky you, because for those who have experienced it first-hand, social anxiety can feel debilitating. To get anxious in situations where, logically, you know you shouldn't creates inner turmoil. Doing 'normal' things like talking to the cashier suddenly feels impossible, and something as simple as going into a crowded shop can make your heart race. When you have social anxiety, you're always comparing yourself to everyone else who seems to sail through life with ease. You start to wonder what is wrong with you – but the reality is, there's nothing wrong with you. It's just your brain trying to keep you safe.

The thing is, no one with social anxiety chooses to have it. The person who is too shy to speak up at meetings desires nothing more than to feel confident sharing their ideas loud and proud.

I have been there; I know how it feels to be crippled by social anxiety, and that is why I am such an advocate for rejection therapy now. It's the only thing that has completely skyrocketed my confidence in such a short amount of time.

**The skills you learn by doing rejection therapy will be skills you have for ever.**

Naturally, like anything, confidence fluctuates. Some days you'll feel unbeatable and other days you'll feel like a shell of yourself – and that's OK. Confidence isn't something that is permanently at a high; it's bound to change, depending on your mood, hormones, stress levels, how much sleep you've had or even how you feel about yourself on that day. Some days you will feel capable, open and ready to take on challenges. Other days you may feel more doubtful, withdrawn or sensitive to judgement. Both are normal parts of being human.

Over the past two years, I've had many fluctuations. I've had periods of time where the desire to keep putting myself in uncomfortable situations has been low. Where I've felt tired of drawing attention to myself. Because of this, I've learned the art of making accommodations. Just because one day I may do a crazy challenge doesn't mean I need to live up to that every other day. In fact, that's a recipe for burnout. I've become very good at listening to my body and using my intuition. If I'm already at capacity, I won't force myself to do something that will only make it worse. Which is why, throughout this book, I encourage you to be in touch with your own needs.

Granted, doing rejection therapy for two years is very different from a thirty-day challenge, so you may not encounter low-capacity days but, if you do, it's OK to listen to yourself.

I started my social-media journey with the aim of helping at least one person, because I'd been through so much turmoil as a teenager. Posting my challenges on TikTok was a way for me to share what I'd learned and what supported me when I felt like I couldn't be helped. My hope was always to reach someone who might be struggling in a similar way. By sharing my rejection therapy journey, those messages have reached millions.

Writing this moment made me unexpectedly emotional. So much so that, as I sit here, looking at my laptop, I find myself tearing up. This journey has truly fulfilled me.

The content I create is what I needed when I was a teenager – it is the content I needed when I was having a really hard time. For me, it's never been about creating pranks or trying to get to the next 'viral moment'. It's as simple as this – my videos have always been rooted in helping people.

One of the most frequent comments I get online is, 'I wish I had your confidence.' It's one I always find interesting because, in my mind: **confidence is a skill anybody can build.**

Confidence isn't something some people are born with and others aren't – it's a skill that absolutely anyone can build. We all have different upbringings and experiences that may shape our confidence, but in this moment, right now, you have the choice whether to take a step forward towards a more confident version of you or stay in your comfort zone.

Where a lot of us go wrong is we feel the discomfort, and take that as a sign that we shouldn't do something. But that is how we limit our growth. Getting nervous isn't a sign not to do it.

**When something scares you, that is when you should do it.**

Circumstances matter – you shouldn't walk into a busy road because it scares you. But when you avoid introducing yourself to new people at an event, don't share your ideas in a group setting out of fear, get nervous at the prospect of starting an exercise class or hobby, can't bring yourself to post on social media, don't tell someone you have feelings for them, hold back on asking for a promotion or pay rise, can't fathom going for a meal alone, and avoid doing anything that feels uncomfortable or new – from volunteering to solo travelling to setting a boundary – that's a sign to start doing things differently. When something feels scary – but you know deep down it actually isn't, it's time to feel the fear and **do it anyway.** Often, moments of hesitation are our greatest moments for

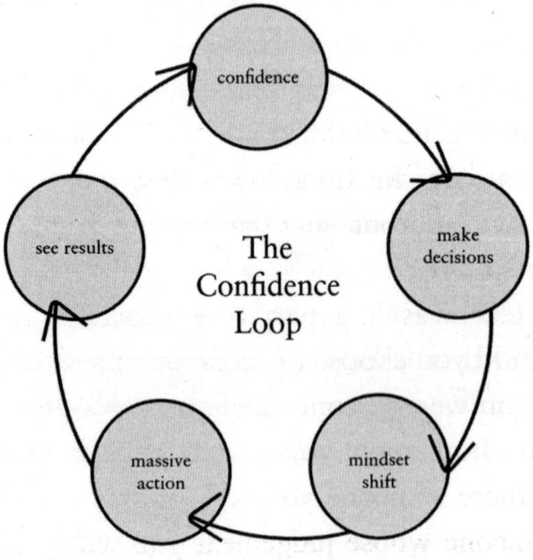

growth. When you feel the fear and do it anyway, that is when your confidence grows.

**You will feel a shift in yourself once you have proved to yourself that you can survive the thing that scared you.** Discomfort is a normal and everyday part of life – and we wouldn't be able to push ourselves out of our comfort zones if we didn't lean into discomfort. When we go beyond our limits, our comfort zones expand, and a byproduct is that our confidence flourishes. And don't we all want that?

Before I leave you to embark on your rejection therapy journey, here are some prompts you can use to identify where rejection is holding you back, and how you can act on this.

**Ask yourself:**

1. Where is fear holding you back in your life?
2. What are the things your heart or soul feel drawn to, but fear has stopped you from pursuing?
3. If fear wasn't a part of the equation, what would you choose to do differently?
4. If you weren't concerned about people's opinions, how might you act or live differently?
5. Is there someone you seek approval from, or someone whose judgement you worry about?

Why does their opinion carry so much weight for you?

6 In what ways does fear shape your decisions?
7 Do you want fear to continue to have this level of control over you – and your life?
8 What is one small action you can take this week to move you slightly closer to the life you want – even if fear is present?

# 15

## A Happier You

If you've made it to this chapter, congratulations!

You've committed to choosing yourself, expanding your mindset and growing your emotional resilience and tolerance to rejection. You've already done the hard part – by picking up this book and reading it.

I hope I've helped to give you the tools you need to see rejection in a different light. Rejection isn't failing and it doesn't reflect your worth. It's a sign of courage – it shows you're striving for more in your life, and that's something to be celebrated.

What I hope you've taken away from this book is that it's not something to fear, nor to avoid. See rejection as a tool to help you get where you want to go in life. Put yourself out there; ask the questions; seek the opportunities; contribute your ideas; start that business; post on social media; give a new hobby a go; wear that outfit.

**By feeling the fear and doing it anyway, you're unlocking a new door in your life.**

It's time to outgrow the old versions of you – to believe in yourself, to have faith that there's more out there for you, and you reading this book is proof of that. You're more courageous, brave and capable than you think, and every time you feel discomfort, it's a sign you're growing. So, seek out discomfort alongside the excitement. Imagine – where might life take you if you stepped into rejection a little more?

**Your next 'no' could be the start of something great.**

Rejection did that for me, and it can for you too. On my journey, I've discovered that rejection has no power unless you give it power. You're always in control of the meaning you place onto rejection. Yes, it stings at times and that's OK. Feel your feelings and hold space for your disappointment but don't stay in that low feeling for ever, because rejection really can be the biggest blessing in disguise. It closes one door so another one opens.

Rejection is a by-product of truly living; you can't control when it will happen, but you *can* control your perspective on it.

Learning how not to fear rejection is how I found my power, built my confidence and overcame my fear to become the person I am today. It transformed my life in more ways I could ever have imagined, and I know it'll do the same for you.

So… it's time to take a deep breath and step into the world of potential rejection.

You've got this; I believe in you.

There are amazing opportunities for you to experience, people you haven't met yet who will change your life, and experiences that exist only on the other side of stepping out of your comfort zone.

It's time to start fully living... the world is waiting for you.

# ACKNOWLEDGEMENTS

Thank you to everyone who has helped make *The Rejection Cure* possible.

I'm so thrilled to be able to share my journey of rejection therapy with you, but this book wouldn't have been possible without these special people.

Firstly, thank you to my manager, Jamie. Thank you for believing in me and for all the behind-the-scenes work to make this book possible. Turns out writing a book is more overwhelming than I expected, so thank you for your consistent, kind support and encouragement to keep me going when things felt hard.

A special mention to Melissa, who's also been a massive support. I'm so grateful to have two thoughtful and amazing managers at Sharp.

Thank you to Mireille, at Bloomsbury, for continuing to always believe in me and make this vision come to life. I am eternally grateful.

Sadé, thank you for helping shape this book, correcting every spelling mistake and sharing your expertise every step of the way.

A massive thank you to everyone at Bloomsbury for believing in my mission and the vision for this book.

And lastly, thank you to you for picking up this book and giving it a read. If you've come from my social media, thank you for the continued support. Every like, follow, message, and comment means the world! I can't wait for you to read this book and help transform your fear of rejection into confidence.

I hope this book helps you as much as writing it helped me.

Sophie x

# INDEX

## A NOTE ON THE AUTHOR

Sophie Jones is a UK-based content creator known for pushing boundaries and embracing the unexpected. Sophie grew to rapid success after her 'Rejection Therapy' series went viral on social media, and has appeared in the *Daily Mail*, Upworthy, and on BBC News and ITV's *This Morning*. She has a combined audience of over 900,000 across Instagram and TikTok.

BLOOMSBURY TONIC

**Tonic**
/ˈtɒn.ɪk/
noun

***A restorative for mind, body and spirit.***
***A spark that lifts, energises and inspires.***
***Something that leaves you feeling better than before.***

At Bloomsbury Tonic, our books are created to nourish you. Each one is intended as a quiet pick-me-up, a steadying presence, and a reminder that feeling better doesn't have to be complicated.

Like any good tonic, these books are designed to invigorate and refresh. They offer new ways of seeing and living, while staying rooted in warmth, honesty and real life. You'll find ideas that are bold and thoughtful, but always human – grounded in experience, compassion and care.

Whether you're turning to this book for comfort, inspiration, practical guidance or a moment of calm, we hope it leaves you feeling restored – a little lighter, a little clearer, and gently energised for whatever comes next.